THE EDUCATION OF AUTONOMOUS MAN

The Education of Autonomous Man

R. T. ALLEN

Avebury

Aldershot · Brookfield USA · Hong Kong · Singapore · Sydney

Published by
Avebury
Ashgate Publishing Limited,
Gower House,
Croft Road,
Aldershot,
Hants GU11 3HR,
England

Ashgate Publishing Company,
Old Post Road,
Brookfield,
Vermont Ø5Ø36,
USA

A CIP catalogue record for this book is available from the British Library and the US Library of Congress.

ISBN 1 85628 381 X

Printed in Great Britain by
Athenaeum Press Ltd, Newcastle upon Tyne.

Contents

Acknowledgements

I wish to thank Harper Collins Publishers for permission to quote from C.S. Lewis' *The Abolition of Man.*

Abbreviations:

Throughout the book, *JPE* = *Journal of Philosophy of Education*

Other abbreviations are explained in the notes at the end of each chapter.

1 The rise of autonomous man

Educational theory has recently regained contact with its past, as can be seen in Professor Bantock's two volumes of *Studies in the History of Educational Thought*, Professor Gordon's and Mr White's *Philosophers as Educational Reformers*, and Professor Peters' *Essays on Educators*. Both positively and negatively there is much to be learned from the past, and we know ourselves only when we know whence we have come. It is especially in respect of fundamental assumptions – about man and the world, human good and destiny, and thus about the general nature and aims of education – that we can learn from the past, rather than about the details of organisation, curricula and methods. For a long time, under the influence of Conceptual Analysis, philosophy of education was closed against the considerations of such questions, and the study of answers to them in the past. But now that metaphysics is once again an accepted part of philosophy, educational theory ought to open itself again to basic issues and thus to review what has already been thought and said about them. Elsewhere I have argued that the pactice and the theory of education inevitably embodies metaphysical assumptions and beliefs, which now ought to be studied [1].

It is the aim of these studies to throw light upon the fundamental assumptions which are made today about the nature of education by examining some selected theorists from the past and by tracing in their work a pattern of variations upon a theme. That theme is the modern conception of the universe, which arose in the seventeenth century, as a world *only* of physical objects in time and space, interacting mechanically as causes and effects according to laws which can be mathematically formulated. It is thus a world of mere things or facts, with only the measurable 'primary' qualities of size and shape, lacking the unmeasurable 'secondary' qualities of colour, taste and smell (which exist only in us as perceivers), and lacking all final causes, purposes, meaning and value. This is the Reductionist view of the world, not that of natural science itself, but that of those who believe that there is *nothing else* to the world than what is formulated in the new physics and chemistry. It is a view first formulated by Galileo and Hobbes [2]. In these

1

studies we shall not be concerned with Reductionism itself but with its effects upon man's view of himself and of his place in the world, and, in turn, with the effects of that view on educational theory.

I shall now briefly summarise some of the principal elements in the new view of the universe and in the consequent views of man, the theme and the variations upon it:

1. The world is now confined to the universe, the system of things in time and space. Already de-divinised and emptied of gods and spirits by Christian theology, it became an autonomous, self-maintaining and closed system of purely natural forces, mechanistic and determinist. It lacks all purpose and teleology. Events happen because of anterior causes and not because of ends to be achieved. The biological realm of plants and animals is viewed in the same way, as can be seen in Descartes' likening of animals to mechanical automata [3].

2. 'Nature' then came to refer to the non-human and untouched, in contrast to the 'artificial', and thus, in the eighteenth century, to the countryside as opposed to the town. It no longer referred to a purposive and normative order which sets a pattern for things and men to follow and achieve. Instead, the nature of something was taken to be simply what it is, and not to be an ideal or complete form of being which has to be achieved. Thus in relation to things human, 'nature' came to refer to the primitive and pre-social. This can be seen in the completely new content give to the notion of Natural Law. Whereas it had referred to a Law above and beyond man, embedded in the very fabric of the cosmos and proceeding from God himself, a Law which all men could and should follow, and which defined the truly human nature that we are not born with but have to achieve, and in achieving find our fulfilment, it then came to refer – in Hobbes, Locke and Rousseau – to what men did, or were supposed to do, in a pre-social and political existence when men were free from social and political restraints on their liberty. True, in Rousseau and Kant there are some lingering notions of Nature as normative, and it seems impossible to rid 'natural' and 'unnatural' of such overtones. But the dominant meaning, within the new view, became that of what merely is the case, especially as untouched by human contrivance. The effects upon education of this change form the main theme of the first volume of Bantock's *Studies*.

3. What then of man himself within the new view of the world? That world, being a closed and mechanical system of mere things without final causes, could no longer present or embody a moral order, and so came to lack all meaning. There cannot be in such a world a Law, Natural or Divine, or Way (*Tao*) for men to follow. Now it has been the assumption of all men in all civilisations that there is such a cosmic order, embodying a Law or Way and being governed by it. It sets man and society a goal to be achieved and a pattern of life to follow, so that to follow that Way and to obey that Law is to become truly human and to find fulfilment, while to stray from or to disobey it is sooner or later to end in disaster. The use of human freedom is to place oneself under that Law or upon that Way, and its abuse is to disobey that Law or to stray from that Way. But the new view of the universe cannot contain any such notions, and so two new understandings of man derive from it:
(a) Man as a self-defining subject in a meaningless universe. Over and against the system of physical things stands the mind or subject who knows it and himself. He is free in the old sense of being able to decide, choose, make initiatives and so be responsible for himself. But now, in a world of mere matter in motion, he is free also in a new sense: viz. radically free or autonomous, for he now has to *think up* his own Law or Way. He has no pre-appointed role in the cosmic drama, for there is none. What drama there is, is a purely human one of which every act performed and word said is improvised by the actors. Men are responsible for themselves but are no

longer responsible *to* anything or anyone above and beyond themselves. Throughout these studies 'autonomous' will be used in this sense, unless where otherwise stated. And it is with this new understanding of man with which we shall be primarily concerned.

(b) Yet, if the world is a closed, mechanical and determinist system, must not man also be a part of it? Instead of free-will and radical freedom, man too is a field of determination by anterior causes, a mechanism. This is Reductionism applied to man himself. Not only is there no Law or Way prior to men's choices, but they could not *choose* to obey or follow it in any case, nor can they choose anything else.

We should note that these two understandings of man are not so contradictory as at first seems, and in Kant, Marx, Helvetius and Skinner we shall see ways in which they are combined. And we should also note that in calling this view of the man and the world (i.e man in a meaningless universe and without a superior Law or Way) the 'new' or 'modern' one, we do not imply (a) that it was entirely without precedent, nor (b) that no other views have arisen since the seventeenth century, nor (c) that it supplanted entirely the older one, which, in the European world, means Christianity.

4. As we shall see, those who accepted the new view of man and the world did not always draw from it all its logical implications. In particular, Deism offered a half-way house between the older view and the new one. Deism retains the notion of God as Creator, and usually as Judge of the dead, but opposes any special interventions on his part into the closed and autonomously functioning world which he has created and set going. That is, it rejects Special Revelation, miracles, the Incarnation and the Church, and relies upon a purely natural or philosophical theology and morality. But the God of Deism, playing no real role in the Deist's life, soon became redundant.

5. As Professor C.Taylor has remarked [4], this new view was represented in the Hellenistic world by Epicureanism, which held the gods to pay no attention to human life, and Scepticism, which denied that we could know the real qualities and effects of our actions. Both left men only with the management of their sensations according to their own wishes. We shall find the Hedonism of Epicureanism revived within several variations of the modern theme.

Even more interesting is the Gnosticism of the Hellenistic world. The various Gnostic systems declared man to be in a state of alienation in this physical world, and were the first to draw a radical distinction between man and the universe [5]. Men are spirits drawn or thrown into this inferior and evil world, and the Gnostic is one who is awakened to this fact and knows both that he belongs to the world of pure spirits and how to get there after death. In the Gnostic view, man is lost and alien in *this* world. Now, without the dramatic mythology of man's previous and future existences, this is the view of man that is found in Heidegger's Existentialism – the analysis of *Dasein* in *Being and Time* but definitely not in later writings – and thus also in Sartre's. And, apart from that particular case, the new view of man is like the Gnostic one in that it too separates man from an alien Nature with which he has nothing in common.

Moreover, men can feel themselves 'thrown', as Heidegger puts it, into the social world, the 'they' and their 'idle talk'. For I as a self-defining subject making my own law for myself find my radical freedom limited from the outside by social and political arrangements into which I am born (or 'thrown'), which I have not chosen and in determining which I have no choice. I have not made myself nor my social, political and cultural situation. Like A.E. Housman, I feel myself to be –

> a stranger and afraid
> In a world I never made.

Here we find the voice of modern Gnosticism. And a few lines later we find its despair in having, unlike the Gnostic of old, no hope of escape:

> But since, my soul, we cannot fly
> To Venus or to Mercury,
> Then keep we must, if keep we can,
> These foreign laws of God and man.

In this way, the autonomy of the self-defining subject issues into a demand for political autonomy – the right to define one's way of life for oneself.

6. At this point the modern world-view divides into its Individualist and Collectivist variants. On the one hand, the emphasis is placed on the solitary individual confronting society and seeking to exercise and safeguard his 'natural rights'. Now the older world-view knew little or nothing of rights and its was a doctrine of Natural *Law*, i.e. duty. But Hobbes, Locke and Rousseau turned the language of 'Natural Law' into one of 'Natural Right', from one of our duties to one in which a moral gloss is put on mere desires and self-assertion [6]. Bentham called all this talk of rights 'nonsense' and that of natural rights 'nonsense on stilts', yet took for granted the right of each to seek his own pleasure in his own way provided that he does not detract from others. And recently this language of natural rights and (political) autonomy has been revived to express the Individualist version of the modern view of man [7]. On the other hand, there arises the Collectivist version *as a logical extension of the Individualist one*. For, finding my radical autonomy limited in its political and social expression by the existence and plans of others, and by the social order in which I have had no say, I can then demand that *we all decide everything together*. In that way, of democratic totalitarianism, we shall intentionally plan the social structure and our lives, rather than each separately negotiate a thousand or more contracts with those others whom we happen to meet. And there is another motive for the shift from Individualism to Collectivism, the yearning of the solitary and alienated soul for a new solidarity in which he can escape from the anguish of isolation. We shall meet several instances of this shift in our studies.

7. There has been one view of the world and man which has arisen in reaction to the modern one yet is not simply a revival of the past: viz. the Romantic conception of the world as organic and expressing a life or spirit within it and thus of man as the potentially self-conscious expression of that life or spirit. As Taylor remarks, that view restored meaning to the world and to human life, yet without any reference to a transcendent Law or Way. Insofar as it personalised that indwelling life or spirit, it was Pantheist and not Theist. It sought to define man, and not to leave him empty and having to define himself, in terms of the indwelling spirit or life of Nature, which man is consciously to express. We shall examine a more Theist form of this reaction in Froebel.

8. There have been other attempts to give man a definition, and so to resolve the dilemmas of self-definition. For example, Rousseau's invocation of devotion to the State insofar as it embodies the general will, that of Marx to define man as a worker, which we shall study, and the usually naive assumptions of Utilitarians that men's motives and desires are directed solely to pleasure and away from pain. We shall examine Utilitarianism in Helvetius and it is employed, as we shall see, by several of our contemporary theorists in order to give a substantive filling to their otherwise empty and Kantian formalism. And we shall review Hegel's ambitious attempt to portray man as the ultimate vehicle of a cosmic *Geist* which is in the process of defining itself. All these attempts, except for Froebel's, operate within a purely mundane framework and without any conception of a superior Law or Way.

9. Another important sub-theme in the development of the modern view, one to be found in nearly all its variations and in the Romantic reaction against it, is that of immanent progress. History never returns to the *status quo ante*, though there are revivals and successful counter-revolutions, for memory makes a difference. Thus loss of Christian belief and hope – of salvation from sin into being made perfect, the vision of God and life eternal – cannot mean a revival of the paganism which it had overcome. For one thing, God as One, transcendent and the Creator, had emptied the world of gods and spirits and their whims, and made it the rational but contingent order which requires empirical and experimental science for men to know it. And, of course, the modern view includes that view of the universe. And, secondly, once having had the hope of a new order of human life – of perfection, men cannot simply revert to the position of those who never had it. Loss of that hope means either a despair deeper than any known by the pagans of old, or the search for a new object for it. Hence arises the 'immanentization of the eschaton', the placing of the End *within* this world and this life, a secularisation of the Christian hope of life eternal. There is a clear historical link between late mediaeval conceptions of the 'millenium', the thousand year rule of the saints before the End of all things along with attempts during the Reformation to realise it, and the new belief in a new order within history towards which it is steadily progressing, or which can be realised by revolutionary effort [8]. Thus arise either beliefs in steady progress to a new and better order of society by the spreading of knowledge and enlightenment, by the casting out of superstition, and by political reforms, or revolutionary and explicitly totalitarian beliefs in the necessity of a Revolution, in which human nature will be transformed, as the threshold to the new order. Either way, the present is the turning point, the crisis, the final darkness before the dawn or the dawn itself.

10. In the revolutionary and totalitarian movements there is a further 'Gnostic' element, the claim by the initiates to have uncovered the secret of history and the plan of its movement from the injustices of the past, through those of the present, to the glorious age at the End. In possession of this knowledge of what has been, what is happening, and what is to come – the secular version of the great Valentinian formula:

> What liberates is the knowledge of who we were, what we became; where we were, whereinto we have been thrown; whereto we speed, wherefrom we are redeemed; what birth is, and what rebirth [9].

The modern Gnostic claims to *know* the movement of history, what men really want, and when and how it will be realised. Thus arise the revolutionary parties and leaders – Robespierre, the Jacobins; the Communist Party, Lenin, Mao, Castro – who claim to embody this knowledge and thus attempt, in Rousseau's fateful words, 'to force men to be free' [10].

11. Finally, we shall note in several theorists an obfuscation of the very issues at stake. For one effect of the new view of man and the universe has been the conclusion, drawn from the success of modern science, that only scientific knowledge is valid. This has led both to attempts to apply such methods to human life as well, which will concern us in the last of these studies, and to the further conclusion that all other claims to knowledge are empty. The name of the latter is Positivism. In particular, Positivism denies the legitimacy of metaphysical knowledge, and dismisses it all as nonsense. But men cannot exist without some view, no matter how vague, of the whole of existence, of the nature of man himself and of man's destiny in the world. And the thesis that all knowledge is contained within the special sciences (those applying to specific regions, aspects or levels of the universe), and especially within the natural sciences, is itself *not* a item of knowledge contained within any of those sciences. It is, eminently, a philosophical and metaphysical thesis. What

Positivists in effect do, is to insinuate their own metaphysics – in the sole reality of the universe (the system of things in time and space) and of this life within it – in dismissing as nonsense any other view because it is metaphysical. We shall therefore review any explicit accounts, given by our chosen theorists, of the nature, scope and possibility of metaphysical knowledge, in order to see how far they are aware of their basic beliefs about the world and man, and thus about the education of men in the world.

Now I have not reviewed these movements of modern thought just to set the scene. For in the following chapters we shall study examples of all these variations and the views of education to which each has led. I have selected the chosen theorists in order to illustrate something of the range of variations on the modern theme.

How, then, will men conceive of education within the new view of man as a self-defining and autonomous subject? That is what we shall study. We shall see that the full implications of the new view are not drawn, as far as concerns education, until our own times. For this there is, I suggest, a general reason – the power of inertia, that for a long time men simply go along with what they have been accustomed to do although their fundamental ideas have changed, and that thus it takes time for them to draw the full implications of a change in their basic beliefs. And there are particular reasons in the case of some of the theorists whom we shall study.

With hindsight, we can see that the principal implication, as far as education is concerned, is that the whole business of education is rendered problematic. In any version of the older view, there are few deep problems about education. Since, in those views, there is a Law which commands us or a Way which summons us, and *to* which we are responsible, then the main task of education is to hand it on to the young and to get them to obey or to follow it as we do ourselves. Indeed, that is part of what it commands or summons us to do. Thus we may slightly alter the familiar injunction from *Proverbs*, in a way with which the author would not have disagreed, to read: 'Train up a child in the *Way* he is to go and he will not depart from it'. But, if we stand under no such Law or Way but have to make up our own, then it is entirely up to us to decide (a) if anything at all be taught to the young and (b), if so, just what. There is now a *problem* of education.

Similarly, under the older view there is, usually, no great problem about the other contents and tasks of education. For example, even with Christianity which is not a new Code (i.e. a prescription of a specific and detailed way of life, as are Judaism and Islam), we can straightforwardly pass our own way of life, unless there is something specifically wrong with it (e.g. slavery), for all fall under God's providence and are *compatible* with the Christian Way. But when men conceive themselves to have to make up all their own laws and ways of life, they are likely to feel, firstly, that sense of Gnostic alienation from the *milieux* into which they find themselves to have been 'thrown', and, secondly, worries and doubts about passing on any way of life to the young and about preparing them for any particular sort of social, political and cultural life. For in the former case, they have not themselves *chosen* the *milieux* into which they are 'thrown', and so resent this fact, and in the latter case they may then be anxious about choosing for the young. Thus we shall expect to find, sooner or later, schemes of education to appear as the result of attempts to circumvent these problems. Alternatively, we may find theorists who are not worried by having to choose for themselves and for the young, either because they are not aware that, on their own assumptions, they are making radical choices, or because they take delight in them.

As a matter of historical fact, although the principal social and political consequences of the new view became apparent by the end of the eighteenth century, many of those for education were not drawn until later, indeed, some until our own times. Consequently we shall find theorists, such as Kant, whose ideas on education, either because of inertia or for particular reasons, show little trace of the new view, which they themselves hold. And we shall also find, in Hegel, a reaction against the social and political consequences, and thus a revision of the new view, which in turn issues in scheme of education which is not radically different from what follows from versions of the older view.

These facts have a methodological significance: viz. that one cannot simply deduce 'implications for education' from general conceptions of man and the world, as the older philosophy of education tried to do. This is not because, as Conceptual or Linguistic Analysis held, that such conceptions, if they are not nonsense in the first place, are in any case irrelevant in the second, but because additional conceptions, beliefs and assumptions at an intermediate level are required as well, such as those about the structure of society, the abilities of children, the relative importance of contemporary activities, the present state of culture, the needs of the times. As we shall see, beliefs on this level can make a significance difference to the ways in which the same fundamental beliefs are worked out in a scheme of education.

In addition, 'deducing the implications for education' is a mistaken method because it assumes that the only relation between fundamental beliefs and assessments of the tasks and nature of education is one of entailment. More frequent, I suggest, are the two neglected relations of permitting and debarring. A world-and-life-view will allow some things in everyday life and thence in education, and will debar others, as well as requiring a third set. This especially true of one which, like Christianity as already mentioned, does not include a specific Code therefore allows many human practices and thence many possible contents of education, while not requiring any one of them. By permitting and debarring, a world-and-life-view acts like a filter rather than a pump. It may therefore appear not to act at all if does not obviously debar things which are currently practised and taught. But, like a filter in relation to clean petrol, it is still there and would debar conflicting beliefs and practices were they to arise.

Because of the necessity of intermediate beliefs and assumptions, I shall not presume to deduce for him any theorist's view of education, though I shall note tensions, lacks of connection and clear contradictions between fundamental conceptions, stated or implied, and statements on education. That is why I have chosen thinkers who both set out, or at least express, a version of the new view of man or a new reaction against it, and also present a scheme of education. The one exception is Sartre, who has only a few, yet very significant, sentences upon education, but who sets forth more clearly and completely than anyone else the new view of man as radically free or autonomous.

We shall keep more or less to a chronological order, and shall then, in the final chapter, bring together the major points of similarity and difference among our chosen theorists in a comparative and critical review of the variations on the modern theme as they issue in conceptions and schemes of education.

One final remark: it will not be every item in a theorist's account of education which will concern us, but only those items which illustrate and clearly follow from his fundamental conceptions of man and the world. For the most part, they will be his views of the general nature and tasks of education, and of its moral and political aspects, and any other items may well be omitted.

Notes

1. See my 'Metaphysics in Education', *JPE*, Vol. 23 No. 2, 1989; 'The Meaning of Life and Education', *JPE*, Vol.25 No. 1, 1991; and 'Reductionism in Education', *Paideusis*, Vol. 5, No. 1, 1991.
2. See M. Grene, 'Hobbes and the Modern Mind' in (ed) M. Grene, *The Anatomy of Knowledge*, and E.A. Burtt, *The Metaphysical Origins of Modern Science*.

3. *Discourse on Method*, p.73.
4. *Hegel*, Chap. 1. I owe to Prof. Taylor the formulation of the new view of man as a self-defining subject in a meaningless universe.
5. See H. Jonas, *The Gnostic Religion*, in particular, pp.160-1 on the appearance for the first time in history, in the *Poimandres* of 'Hermes Trismegistus', of the radical difference between man and nature; p.166, also in the *Poimandres* of the stripping of from the self of all its empirical characteristics to reveal the pure self that existed before its fall in this world (compare, in Chaps. 4, 5 and 7 below, the desire on the parts of Marx and contemporary philosophy of education to liberate men from the conditions of finite existence, Hegel's attempt to reconcile men to them, and Sartre's despairing conclusion that no such liberation is possible); and the Epilogue on the Gnostic parallel in Heidegger's *Being and Time.*
6. On the great difference between the theory of Natural Law theory and the modern one of Natural Right, see Leo Strauss, *Natural Right and History.*
7. R. Nozick's *Anarchy, State, Utopia* is a contemporary statement of the wholly individualist version, while J. Rawls' *A Theory of Justice* is a contemporary statement of the version in which individuals negotiate a collective arrangement (to secure equality of condition).
8. See N. Cohn, *The Pursuit of the Millenium.*
9. Clement of Alexandria, *Excerpts from Theodotus* 78.2, quoted Jonas, op. cit., p.45.
10. On the Gnostic elements in modern philosophy and political theory, and on the 'immanentization of the eschaton', see Eric Voegelin, *Science, Politics and Gnosticism* and *The New Science of Politics.* See also J. Talmon, *The Origins of Totalitarian Democracy.*

2 Rousseau: From alienation to totalitarian democracy

In Rousseau we find the solitary self alienated from society yet dreaming of escaping into a new solidarity of totalitarian democracy. We find this in his life, his writings and his views of education. Curiously, as regards education attention has been fixed upon *Emile* and the withdrawal of the self and the child from society, and the supposed freedom allowed to the child; whereas, with regard to politics, attention has been fixed on the *Social Contract* and the passage from the solitariness of each in the pre-social state of nature to solidarity of all in 'the general will' as embdied in the social contract. It is time to bring these two sides of Rousseau together.

Formally, Rousseau was a Deist, of a sentimental sort in contrast to the dry rationalism of Voltaire. This world-view we find expressed in the 'Creed of a Savoyard Priest' in *Emile* and in Book IV, Chap. VIII, 'Civil Religion' of the *Social Contract* [1].

In the former, we find a creed based only on natural reasoning and with but three articles: belief in God, based on the argument from motion in the universe to the Will which set the universe in motion; belief in God's wise governance of the universe, from the design and harmony found in the universe; and the freedom of the human will and the self as immaterial. The soul is said to be probably immortal. These articles for only a natural religion and Rousseau specifically opposes the idea of a Special Revelation by God – i.e. one at a particular time and place to or through particular men – and thus the historic, authoritative and institutional religion consititued by it.

This natural religion is, we may say, epiphenomenal: that is, it plays no active part in Rousseau's thinking, just as in the Deist conception God created the universe and left it to run on by itself according to the laws with which he has endowed it and so plays no further part in it. For in the same place Rousseau states that the principles of human conduct, justice and virtue, are innate and to be found in one's own heart or conscience and consist in 'following nature'. But 'following Nature' in Rousseau can mean only doing what Nature permits, i.e what is physically possible (cf. *E* p.6), and by 'virtue' he primarily means the devotion of the citizen to the common good,

9

and this, as we shall see, does not follow from any Law superior and prior to human choice. And so, despite some indications to the contrary, Rousseau does express the modern view of man. Moreover, conscience, a matter of feeling rather than judgment, is said to be infallible. Thus it cannot be an interior witness to a Law which exists independently of the individual. And men's first impulses are said to be always good: 'Oh, let us leave man unspoilt; he will always find it easy to be good and he will always be happy without remorse' (*E* p.256). This clearly rules out any need for divine illumination and redemption. It also is implied that man's end and happiness lies in this life and this world. Moreover, in his own voice, Rousseau presents this Creed, not as a rule for belief, but as an example how one should reason with the adolescent pupil. Human reason can yield only this natural (unrevealed) religion, and only that wuld be taught to Emile. 'If he must have any other religion, I have no right to be his guide; he must choose for himself (*E* p.278). This foreshadows our contemporary theorists of rational autonomy, who, however, have much less faith in reason and would deny that it can conclude to God's existence, and who therefore require pupils to be allowed to choose much more for themselves. Personally, this natural religion is only a matter of intellectual assent and requires no re-orientation of one's life in its light.

Socially and politically matters are somewhat different. In the *Social Contract* Rousseau argues that the idea of a spiritual kingdom, not of this world, makes a good polity impossible in Christian states – that is, it sets God over and against Caesar and divides men's allegiances. Such is 'priestly religion' which gives men two laws, two rulers and two countries. It is worthless in breaking the unity of society and setting man against himself. Rousseau commends Hobbes for seeing the way out, a unitary authority (i.e. Caesar) who will determine religious and well as political life. Therefore he distinguishes, and sets against 'priestly religion', *private religion*, which is a purely interior cult of an omnipotent God and the eternal duties of morality, a divine natural law, from *civic religion*, an external cult prescribed by the law of the land, a positive divine law. The latter is good as making (as among the ancient Greeks) one's country the object of adoration, but can be bad when founded on lies and when blood–thirsty and intolerant. As for the former, pure Christianity adds nothing to the force of the laws of the state and detaches men from the world, and so nothing is more contrary to the social spirit. Conversely, by preaching servitude and dependence it is too favourable to tyranny. Therefore he recommends the establishment, by the sovereign who is comptent to decide what touches on public utility, a civic faith which the citizens have not to oppose, to which they must conform their behaviour, but which they need not believe in their hearts. This civic faith is to have only the simple dogmas, without gloss or commentary, of belief in God and his providence, personal immortality and judgment after death, and 'the sanctity of the social contract and the laws', plus also the negative dogma of forbidding intolerance (*SC* p.153). Now the point of this civic religion is not that it is true and can be shown to be true but that it makes good citizens: that is, by believing it or by acting as if they did, they will behave better towards each other and towards the state. (As Voltaire said, if God did not exist he would have to be invented – in order to make men behave in this world by threatening them with punishment and encouraging them with rewards in the next.) On the other side, any religion claiming to present the one way of salvation breaks up the peace and cannot tolerate others. Therefore all other religions are to be tolerated so long as they do not make exclusive claims. Hence Robespierre, the Revolutionary leader who most closely followed Rousseau and who claimed to embody the general will, insisted on the establishment of this civic religion, set up in Notre Dame a cult of a prostitute, representing the goddess of Reason, and required the elimination of any who would not accept it.

So, then, Rousseau in effect presents man as radically autonomous, and makes religion either ineffective or a function of the state. And in the movement of return to society we find shall the desire to have the laws and institutions society determined by everyone together so that they embody the will of each, and thus are not just given to the citizen willy-nilly. And we shall find in his writing another effect of the new cosmology: man as alienated from society and then seeking, as we have just seen, solidarity with others in this life and this world, a solidarity to which religion must be adapted or be banished. Or, perhaps, what we find is Rousseau's own isolation and his compensatory dream wherein he vicariously satisfies his yearning for community. Either way, his writings on politics and education provide us with a statement of two significant variations modern theme, and of the oscillation between them.

We begin with the individual's alienation from society. In his *Discourses* Rousseau had appeared to reject civilization. But it is a simpler and uncorrupted state of civilization which he invokes, not a return to a pre-social and pre-cultural 'state of nature'. Now whether or not it was a projection of his own temperament, Rousseau regarded the society of his time as corrupt. That he makes clear in the opening pages of *Emile*. Therefore the retreat from society is, overtly, a tactical one in order that Emile may grow up uncorrupted, and then later rejoin it with no or little risk of infection, rather than a rejection of social existence as such. But Rousseau's attitude to civilization is highly ambiguous, apart from his rejection of his own times. This shows up in his conception of nature. The state of nature is a pre-social life; nature within us is our innate dispositions before they are changed; and Nature is beyond our control – in education, the maturation of our organs and faculties (*E* pp.6–7). That is, nature is the pre-human and primitive, both as 'first' and as 'undeveloped'. Therefore he contrasts the natural man, in this sense, who lives for himself with the product of civilization. But he defines good social institutions as those which will make men 'unnatural', that is, to make men dependent upon one another and not solitary, so that the individual is merged into the group and each regards himself only as part of the whole and thinks only of its common life in which he shares (*E* p.7). Yet two pages later, having declared the education for social life as set out in the *Republic* to be impossible today, Rousseau contrasts the fixed stations of men in the social order, and the alignment of education to prepare the young for them, with the equality of men in the natural order where they have a common calling – manhood. The primitivist strain is dominant and called forth Edmund Burke's protest that 'Art is man's Nature' and that the Apollo of Belvedere is a much a representation of human nature as are the rustic clowns of Rembrandt and Teniers.

As a consequence, Rousseau falls a victim to the fallacy of the abstract universal. Nature has called us to be men, and to to fill any specific roles. 'Life is the trade I would teach him......In vain will fate change his station; he will always be in the right place' (*E* p.9). That is, Rousseau would have Emile trained for no particular place in society so that he can fill any. Again, Emile as to be considered only as a 'man in the abstract' or in general and not as a particular person in a particular and changing situation (*E* p.1∅).

Rousseau might just have well said that Emile should not be taught French or German but just language. Another version of the same fallacy, and one originated by Rousseau [2], is that of not teaching children anything definite but instead getting them to 'learn how to learn'. But, more importantly, these passages show a rejection of the finitude of man: that in being and doing one thing we forego the possibility of being and doing other things, what economists call 'opportunity cost'. And, I suggest, they reveal that resentment of being thrown into roles and relationships which one has not chosen. 'All his life long man is imprisoned by our institutions' (*E* p.1∅); 'We were meant to be men, laws and customs thrust us back into infancy' (*E* p.49); Emile 'does not know the meaning of habit, routine and custom' (*E* p.125). But man without institutions, laws, customs, habits and routines, is no longer man. What Rousseau, like the miser, seems to desire is the abstract and total freedom of pure potentiality, which hovers above concrete options and which is lost when one chooses to do something, something specific and thus not other things. With regard to roles and relationships, this desire for absolute freedom manifests itself as a resentment at being limited by them – by being a nurse and therefore *not* a doctor or engineer, or even by being a woman and not a man. It resents and rejects differentiation, and so desires uniformity but an abstract and empty one which, not being anything specific, is not being anything at all. We shall meet it again in Marx and Sartre.

In *Emile* Rousseau contrasts dependence on men and dependence on things, and wishes Emile's education to be the latter. But, of course, Emile will be very dependent on his tutor, though he will not realise it. And Rousseau, unlike his child-centred followers, is explicit about that. So it is not dependence on men in itself that he rejects, and, were he to do so, Emile would have to be cast out of society altogether. What he rejects is what he considers to be the present state of corruption whereby the individual comes to live by the desire to cut a good figure in the eyes of others or by comparisons of himself with them. These are unnatural passions of *amour propre* – selfishness and pride. In contrast, *amour de soi* is a natural passion which is the means to freedom and self-preservation (*E* 173–4). As we shall see, Helvetius drew a similar distinction. But the *amour de soi* is St Augustine's *amor sui*, which is what must be broken by the grace of God if man is to attain his true end and fulfilment. But Rousseau and Helvetius have lost any, or any significant, reference to Transcendence, and take men purely as they happen to be, or, in Rousseau's case, also as they were or would have been in a pre-civilized state of nature [3]. Moreover, if men are born good, and their first impulses always right (*E* p.56), then the mere juxtaposition of one man with another will not cause evil thoughts and attitudes to arise in either. And, if the mere presence of the other is sufficient to arouse pride and selfishness, then the only effective remedy would be a permanent withdrawal of Emile from human society.

Emile is to be taught dependence only on things, and not to command and obey, and this in childhood. His unreasonable desires are to be countered by physical obstacles and the punishment of natural consequences: that is, he is to be prevented, physically prevented, from doing wrong, and not to be verbally forbidden. It is thus necessary to distinguish his natural from his artificial needs – that is, respectively, those which he can carry out for himself and those which he cannot – and to meet only the former. He is to get only what he (naturally) needs, and not what he asks, and is to act from necessity and not obedience (*E* pp.49–53).

Unlike his child-centred followers, Rousseau is well aware of the dangers of spoiling children. Hence Emile is not to be indulged, although no commands or prohibitions will be spoken to him. In addition, he has a clearer view than our contemporary theorists have of the dangers of reasoning with children: they do not understand the language used and they will come to 'question all that is said to them, to think themselves as wise as their teachers; you train them to be argumentative and rebellious' (*E* p.53). We shall find the same robust opinion in Hegel. But, later on, when he is twelve, Emile is to discover science for himself, and not be *told* so that he does not depend on authority but only on reason and therefore avoids being the 'plaything of people's thoughts' (*E* p.131). But it is clear throughout the book that, although the tutor never *tells* Emile what to do and what not to do, nor tells him much at all, he nevertheless determines, by his unseen manipulations of the things around Emile, what Emile will learn, do, feel and become. In adolescence, when he rejoins society and has to cope with women and his feelings towards them, he will, Rousseau hopes, be fully under his tutor's control because he will now obey from his own free will (*E* p.298).

Although Rousseau is hostile to civilization and its arts and sciences, he realises that men can never revert to the state of nature, and were Emile to remain in that state, when others have left it, he would be isolated and wretched (*E* p.156). Consequently, Emile is to study things – things and not words – and to learn

12

practical science so that he can be his own D–I–Y man like Robinson Crusoe, the one book he is to be allowed to read before adolescence. Man's proper study is not man but his relation to the natural world (*E* p.175). But he must, at this period, begin to study men, from afar and in the abstract, and to learn to love them and pity them. He will then study their differences and the inequalities of society. He will know that they are good by nature but corrupted by society (*E* pp.184–9).

Rousseau thus has no inhibitions about prescribing a definite ideal for what sort of person Emile is to become, the means to realise it, and the contents of all aspects of his education. There is precious little about autonomy here. But I think that we can nevertheless see the influence of the new view of man and the world in Rousseau's distrust of civilization.

But, if Emile is reluctantly returned to society after being innoculated against it, when Rousseau contemplates a unified society, he appears to have few reservations. While the declared intention of the *Social Contract* shows that same mistrust of the state which in Hobbes, Locke and the whole of Liberalism descending from them, makes it a necessary evil, Rousseau goes into raptures over the devotion to the common good over private concerns which he thought to have been displayed in republican Rome. The aim of the *Social Contract* is to set out a form of association which wil protect each individual and his property and in which each citizen 'while joining with all the rest, still obeys no one but himself, and remains as free as before' (*SC* pp.14–5). That is the problem. The former part echoes Locke and Anglo-American Liberalism, but the latter inaugurates the Continental dream of totalitarian democracy. For the answer to the problem is Rousseau's version of the social contract, in which all individuals will totally alienate themselves and their rights to the community as a whole. Because all will do this, they are all equals in and under the social contract, and so it will not pay anyone to make it a burden to the rest (*SC* p.15). Rousseau's position is like Hobbes' in that he makes the social contract one among all the members of the state which it brings into existence and in that he makes it a total alienation of them all to the sovereign, and so unlike Locke's wherein it is a treaty between the people and the sovereign who is separate from them and wherein they reserve the right to revoke it. But in Rousseau's social contract, the sovereign is never distinct from the totality of members and is them acting in their corporate capacity. But these are minor differences among the three theorists. Far more important is their fundamental unanimity in basing the state upon the will of individuals to secure their own persons and property and the derivation of all law, right and legitimacy from this self-centred will, and *not*, as in Natural Law theory, from those unwritten laws of which Antigone speaks, which exist prior to all human will and to which the individual and the state ought to conform.

The social contract includes a tacit agreement, on which everything else rests, that anyone who refuses to obey the general will shall be forced to do so by the whole body, 'which means nothing more or less than that he will be forced to be free' (ominous words!). Because all give themselves to the state, they are freed from subservience to any particular persons, and only this contract can give legitimacy to all civic obligations 'which otherwise would be absurd, tyrannical, and subject to the gravest abuses' (*SC* p.19). Rousseau clearly expresses the Liberal view that obligations arise only from our own choices and as we voluntary incur them – that none exist prior to any contracts, explicit or implicit, which we make, and so all take the form of keeping our promises. He also clearly expresses the view that legitimacy derives solely from consent. But on the older view, positive law, the actual law of any state, is law only as it reflects, or is not incompatible with, what Plato called 'the right laws'. Rousseau's politics are definitely those of the new cosmology and anthropology.

Rousseau's great problem is to pass from this abstract principle – the will of each to be 'all for one and one for all' – to concrete polities, constitutions and policies. It would appear that only in a small and participatory democracy, where each votes in person, can the general will emerge. Moreover, it seems that it can emerge only from unanimous decisions: it must both proceed from all and apply to all (*SC* p.32). Even then the people may be mistaken or deceived, and so their real will – the general will – will not be expressed in what they actually will. This means that the general will cannot be simply identified with 'the will of all' (*SC* pp.4∅, 114). Yet he asserts that unanimity applies only to the formation of the social contract, at which time those who oppose it become foreigners to the state thereby constituted, and not thereafter (*SC* p.117). It is, of course, a matter of dispute how far Rousseau regarded his social contract as an historical fact (like Locke) or as an explanatory, and justifying myth or model (like Hobbes). Really to legitimate government on the basis of each subject's will, it would have to be historical. In any case, Rousseau has to legitimize the practice of majority rule after the social contract. All he can offer is the argument that, if I find myself in the defeated minority and so bound against my will, I am not really bound against my will for I simply made a mistake as to what the general will is, so that, had my opinion prevailed, I would then have been voting for what I do not (really) intend. He comments that this assumes that 'all the characteristics of the general will continue to be found in the majority' (*SC* p.118). But that qualification either totally negates the utility of majority rule or is of no consequence. Rousseau can never tell us what the general will is in any concrete case or how to determine it. It remains merely formal and indeterminate, a merely abstract universal like language as such and as opposed to any actual language, or becomes identified with the will of whoever claims to embody it – a majority or, more usually, a party, such as the Jacobins, or a leader such as Robespierre. It then justifies everything and anything, since it is by definition right and infallible (*SC* pp.28, 114) [4]. That is how radical individualism passes into totalitarian tyranny, against which no one can raise a legitimate complaint for he is complaining against the general will and therefore his own will, which is now 'forcing him to be free'.

The ambiguity of Rousseau's attitude to society and civilization continues in the *Social Contract*. On the one hand, especially in Bk III, he shows contempt towards actual people and policies, and, on the other, he idolizes the patriotism of the ancient Romans and yearns for the ideal of total unanimity in the devotion of all to the common good, which he terms the general will.

It is manifest that something quite different from the education of Emile is required for the general will to emerge and to prevail. And in his *Considerations on the Government of Poland* Rousseau briefly indicates the education that would be needed, one which will give the young a 'national formation' and so direct their opinions and tastes that they will be 'patriotic by inclination, by passion, by necessity', so that they will see nothing but their fatherland from birth to death (*CGP* p.176). The state is clearly to be their God, the sole object of their devotion, and obviously all aspects of education would have to be directed towards that end. Rousseau gives only a few details in specification of this education. He states that the young should learn the history, geography and laws of their country between the ages of 12 and 16; that education should be regulated by law; that all the young should be educated in the same way; that physical education is important in preventing vices from arising; and that children's play should be communal and public, so that they become accustomed to rules, equality, fraternity, competition and living under the eys of their fellow citizens, as well as becoming fit and agile (*CGP* pp.176-9). Even these few details indicate an education totally different in character, aim and content, from that prescribed for Emile. For now Rousseau is prescribing an education, and a constitution, for what he takes to be a free and uncorrupted people.

Rousseau and his schemes of education therefore oscillate between, on the one hand, rejection of, retreat from and reluctant return to actual society, and, on the other, enthusiastic yearning for and dedication to a merging of all separate individuals into one mind and one will for the common good, which he conveniently places at a safe distance – in ancient Rome or in contemporary Poland. One may indeed wonder if, in the last resort, Rousseau would only reluctantly accept any actual society and government, no matter how close to his ideal. What we do not find in his politics and schemes of education, save only in Emile's return to a society to which he does not really belong and against which he has been innoculated, is an education for a set of individuals each to determine his own way of life and so to negotiate it that he obstructs as little as possible the ways determined by others – the standard Liberal view of politics and education. It is either the alienated individual versus society or the merging of the individual into one general will, which occupies his attention [5]. We shall find the same movement in Sartre. In both cases, there is no Law or Way superior to the individual, either as isolated or as giving himself over to the general will, which would prescribe obligations, a way of life and a mode of education for him.

Notes

1. References to Rousseau's works will be given in the text using the following abbreviations:
   CGP = *Considerations on the Government of Poland*;
   E = *Emile*;
   SC = *The Social Contract.*
2. Emile is not to be taught the natural sciences but is to learn the methods of learning them, *E*, p.135.
3. See below, p.66.
4. Talmon, *Origins*, quotes in an Appendix several passages from Robespierre, and their sources in Rousseau, wherein he claims to embody the general will. Talmon shows how both use 'definitional thinking' by which to make their propositions true by means of stipulative definitions which change from one statement ot the next and so render the argument fallacious. This sort of thinking is the result of an attempt to pass from an ideal which cannot be realized in human affairs to concrete institutions and policies supposedly embodying it.

3 Kant and Froebel: Autonomy of the will and cosmic expression

There is little that is original in Kant's own work on education (his last published work) and it reflects nothing of his later political thought, which takes up ideas from Rousseau and expresses the hopes of the Enlightenment for progress to a better state for man on earth [1]. Nor does it directly reflect what is original in his moral philosophy. But his general philosophy, and especially his moral philosophy, focus many themes of interest to us and are an important point of reference for the later philosophers whom we shall study. Moreover it is interesting to see how Kant, from his version of man as a self-defining subject, concludes to a fairly conventional view of education.

We begin with Kant's later and 'critical' philosophy, in which he rejected the rationalistic metaphysics of his earlier period, derived from Christian Wolff and thence from Leibnitz and Descartes, and originated significant elements of the later Positivist dismissal of all metaphysics. The chief work of the Critical philosophy is the *Critique of Pure Reason* but easier access to its themes is provided by the *Prolegomena to Any Future Metaphysics.* Kant was led by Hume and his own discovery of the 'antinomies of reason' to revise his former idea of metaphysics as an attempt to give a deductive and *a priori* account of Reality, and especially of the freedom of the will, the immortality of the soul as a simple substance, and the existence of God. He still held to that idea of metaphysics but greatly restricted its scope.

He completed the Cartesian turn by founding metaphysics upon epistemology (theory of knowledge), and so inaugurated what he called a 'Copernican revolution' in philosophy [2]. Instead of regarding the necessity thought to be in causal laws, as founded upon Nature itself, he argued that it is prescribed to Nature by the mind itself (36). For us to have experience, he argued, it is necessary both that perception give us sensory intuitions and that the understanding relate them by means of concepts, which it itself generates (18). The pure concepts employed by the understanding such as substance and causation are therefore also univeral laws of nature which can be known *a priori* (22). But what we know as Nature is not 'things in themselves' ('noumena') but only 'appearances' ('phenomena'). The former remain for ever unknown and unknowable. All that we know and can know is things as they appear to us and thus as conforming to the pure concepts of the understanding (19). Hence propositions such as that substance is permanent and every event has a cause, are known to be necessarily and universally true , for they express laws which the understanding prescribes to experience (25–36). Such laws could not be gleaned from experience since they go beyond it (14).

Yet the human mind is not constituted by perception and understanding only, but also by reason which operates with pure concepts alone and apart from experience. This is the sphere of metaphysics whose concepts therefore cannot be affirmed about real objects (40). They are not needed for, and would get in the way of, a science of Nature (that is, Newton's physics and a psychology modelled on it). They represent an ideal of complete knowledge, beyond experience and about things in themselves, which is impossible for us (46, 57). And 'the antimonies of reason' pairs of contradictory propositions about the world as whole, freedom of will, and the existence of God show, Kant concluded, that there we are dealing only with appearances (51–2b). And arguments for the existence of God also show that we mistake an hypothesis for a definite assertion (55) [3]. But we can also learn from the antimonies, not only not to go beyond experience, but that experience is not everything, though we can never know what else there is (57). We therefore conclude that materialism, naturalism and fatalism cannot be proved to apply to things in themselves (60).

This makes it possible, on moral grounds, not to affirm that the will is free, the soul immortal, and God to exist, but practically to postulate such things. These arguments are presented in the *Critique of Pure Reason* (A806–819, B834–847) and *Critique of Pure Practical Reason* (Bk II, Chap. II) [4]. We do not know that we are not free and not immortal and that God does not exist, and so we can postulate that we are free and immortal and that God does exist because the moral law requires freedom and endless approximation to the ideal of freedom which we can never reach, and would be null and void, although it commands irrespectively of consequences, if God did not exist to join disinterested virtue with the happiness which it deserves. But we cannot affirm that in reality we are free and immortal and that God does exist.

We note that God is not, in Kant's philosophy, the object of man's endeavours, as he is in Platonic and Christian thought. That would constitute 'heteronomy' of the will, seeking a good for a reason other than the abstract and formal command to do one's duty just because it is one's duty. This brings us to Kant's moral philosophy, the chief points of which were presented in his *Groundwork of the Metaphysics of Morals*.

Kant begins by observing that the only thing which is good without qualification is a good will talents, temperament and gifts of fortune can be both good and bad (p.59). And a good will is good through its willing alone, its disinterestedness, and not because of any effects which it may happen to have (p.60). That means that it does its duty because it is its duty, and does not merely conform with duty for some other motive (p.63). That again means that action from duty has its worth only in the 'maxim' or principle involved (p.65). Thus the motive for duty is reverence for duty and never the result expected, and thus it is the idea of the moral law as such (p.66). That yields Kant's famous Categorical Imperative, that 'I ought never to act except in such a way *that I can also will that my maxim should become a universal law*'. It is bare conformity to universal law as such which must be the principle of the will (p.67). All duty is contained in what has become known as the principle of universalisability: that the maxim of one's action should be capable of being a universal law (p.68).

Kant thus seeks to derive the whole duty of man from the idea of the rational will, whether or not any actual will exemplifies it or, rather, from the form of a

17

rational will, universal law. In the *Groundwork* he derives some duties from it. One of the most important of these is the command to treat humanity, in oneself and others, always as an end and never just as a means (pp.9Ø-1). And he sought to derive more in the *Metaphysics of Morals*, all by pure deduction from the form of a universal law which can be rationally willed. As rational and as following the formal requirements for a rational will, the will is subject to and creates the moral law, a law binding upon and legislated in the same way by all rational wills (p.93). Any other source of duty would be, in Kant's eyes, 'heteronomous'. The moral law, and thus the rational will which legislates it, must be 'autonomous' and not take duty from elsewhere. Hence there is no Natural Law or Way above man for men to follow, nor would it have moral authority if there were. Man, we may say, is in Kant's view a self-legislating subject as and only as rational will following the form of universal law and what is strictly deduced from it. That is, as he may be 'in himself', though in 'inner perception' and natural science he appears to be but a part of a Nature causally determined throughout. Thus we find in Kant elements of both the basic types of anthropology of the modern outlook.

Many criticisms have been made of both Kant's methods and conclusions in ethics, and some we shall meet later [5]. We note now one of the most common that all his Categorical Imperative can yield are duties not to do things which cannot be universal laws, and never any positive actions. We also note, with Max Scheler [6], that Kant conflates *values* with *goods* or the things which bear values. Hence he omits the possibility that one can pursue the latter, not just out of (self-centred) 'inclinations', but also from disinterested cherishing of the values instantiated by them, and so he falls back upon the abstract form of universal law. It would appear that for Kant men's inclinations are merely animal appetites and the world a set of things grey and neutral in themselves. Hence imititation of God or men has no place in morality, save only to show what is possible (pp.73, 1Ø4).

We now turn to Kant's theory of education and the educational consequences of his metaphysics and ethics. A dilemma follows from the last point: how can the young learn their duty if imitation can play no part in it and if they are autonomously and rationally to legislate it for themselves? To this Kant gives an answer in Part II of the *Critique of Pure Practical Reason*. It is important to note that Kant always assumed that the commonly recognised duties of human life (what others would call the content of Natural Law) could be strictly deduced from his Categorical Imperative [7]. Thus he held that the young can be formally taught sets of duties, a moral catechism, and then be led to perform them out of the motive of duty for duty's sake. To that end he recommended the use of biographies and stories, as about a man whom others vainly try to persuade, by bribes and threats, to caluminate an innocent and powerless person like Ann Boleyn. The spectacle of his resistance despite all the consequences can inspire the young ardently to desire have the same character and thus to fear above all appearing contemptible in their own eyes. And their judgment can be sharpened by questioning about examples of moral actions, the laws involved and whether or not they were performed from duty.

Similarly in his short work, *On Education*, he can recommend that parents teach such ordinary duties and then later get the young to see their reasonableness for themselves (p.83). And generally we find there conventional advice about the up-bringing of the young, because he assumes that his principles underwrite traditional morality. And so he stresses the need for:

formation of character (p.7ff); instilling of truthfulness (p.92) and sociableness (p.92); encouragement of a cheerful and open-hearted disposition (p.92); discouragement of vanity (p.94); ability to form and keep to resolutions and to go without what one cannot have (pp.97-9); placing before the young duties which they can perform (common ones to self and others) by example and rules (pp.1Ø3-4); a catechism of right conduct in the form of everyday questions and examples (pp.1Ø3-4); cultivation of frankness and unassuming confidence in oneself (p.1Ø6);

18

the control of cravings so that they do not become vices, and a list of vices and virtues (pp.1Ø6-8); and not estimating the gifts of fortune too highly (p.1Ø9).

All that is sound sense, and we note the absence of that agonising over prescriptions for the young which is such a feature of our contemporary theory, which has lost Kant's beliefs in the rational basis of ordinary conceptions of duty.

As for methods, Kant recommends:

direct instruction, example, the giving of a set plan to the child and that he make one and keep to it (p.85); punishment for all transgressions but without anger lest it be seen merely as the result of anger, and 'moral' punishments such as expressions of contempt (which work upon the child's desire to be honoured and loved) and physical ones only to supplement the former (pp.87-9); and competitive games as a release from the restraints of school so as not to quench youthful jollity (p.94).

We see that Kant has a fairly clear idea of what sort of person should be produced and how one should go about producing him. The same applies to those other aspects of his scheme of education which we have omitted.

There are two other points yet to be noted:

(a) The enlarged role given to religion, more in line with Kant's own attitudes than with his explicit philosophy. Religion is still interpreted as wholly a matter of morality [8], but conscience is said to be of no effect if it is not also regarded as the voice of God. Children are to learn to reverence God as the Lord of life and the whole world, and thus to respect God's care for animals (pp.113-4).

(b) Kant's sharing of the Enlightenment's enthusiasm for grandiose schemes of reform so as to produce heaven on earth. Thus children are to be educated, not only for today, but also for 'a possibly improved condition of man in the future, that is in a manner which is adapted to the *idea of humanity* and the whole destiny of man'. Therefore the basis of education must be cosmopolitan and aimed at 'the universal good and the perfection to which man is destined' (pp.14-5).

We note in that last sentence, as also is to be found in 'On Eternal Peace', the idea of Nature as normative and as having designs for man. Kant, it seems, had to bring in something seemingly 'heteronomous' in order to underpin his belief in a definite good and duty for man. While his basic assumptions in philosophy represent mostly the new outlook, his personal religion and his assumption that his ethics coincide with and underwrite traditional morality together yield a mostly conventional view of education. We shall see a similar combination in Hegel, but first we turn to Froebel and the Romantic reaction against the modern cosmology.

Kant divides man into the knowable and phenomenal self which is just another piece of the determinist mechanism that is the universe, and the unknowable and noumenal self which freely determines itself in accordance with the Categorical Imperative which his rational will legislates for itself. This bifurcation of man, and the whole mechanist view of the universe, was rejected by German Romanticism. Even Kant, though officially regarding notions of design and purpose in biology as useful fictions, came to credit Nature with purposes for man. But Herder, the initiator of the new movement of thought, conceived of man wholly in terms of *expression*, individually and collectively [9]. Each person and each nation has its own way of being human, which lies within the person or the nation and is not imparted by the world. And the realization of what lies potentially within reveals it, makes it clear and determinate, and so knowable by the person or nation. As with expression in language and art, all expressiomn is the clarification of a meaning through its embodiment, a meaning that cannot be known before it is expressed. Thus final causes and holistic conceptions are restored, but in the context of a continuance of the idea of self-defining subjectivity. With the Romantic movement, man becomes again a whole person and is no, longer partitioned, as we saw in Kant's view, between reason and animality, for self-awareness is self-feeling, and so feeling is

19

inseparable from thought. And, whole in himself, man is also seen at one with Nature, but in terms of expression and not of following a Law or Way external to man and governing both. Mechanistic views of man and the world are attacked; freedom is seen as authentic self-expression; and one life is seen as flowing through man and Nature, so that men feel themselves to be united with each other and with Nature. Romanticism first went through a Pantheistic phase, in which Nature was held to be an all-inclusive world with God or Spirit wholly in it, and then a more Theistic one in return to Christian belief, yet still with distinctively Romantic elements. It is to that later phase that Froebel belongs, a movement which, as we shall see, Hegel opposed.

Froebel brings into educational theory some of the themes of German Romanticism. Behind the universe is a living unity, all pervading, self-cognisant and ever-lasting, which is God, from whom everything has emanated and in and through whom it has its being. Everything has a purpose: to realise its essence, 'the divine nature developing within it', and thus to manifest God in this world. As a self-conscious being, man is intended to become aware of his essential nature, and 'to reveal the divine element within him by allowing it to become freely effective in his life'. Education should therefore stimulate men to realise their nature and show them how to achieve it. It must make man 'consciously accept and freely realise the power which activates him' and 'perceive and know the divine as it is manifested in his natural surroundings', apprehend the same laws in Nature and himself, see both as proceeding and conditioned by God, and thus to be peace with Nature and united with God [10].

Here we see that meaning is restored to the universe and to human life within it, as expressions of the divine spirit, and thus a task and a Way is set before man, or, rather found within him: consciously to express in his life the divine spirit. The universe is not just the cosmic clockwork of Newtonian science, or what was taken to be such. But, paradoxically, man is already made and defined just as he is in the Reductionist applications of physics to human life. The freedom which Froebel requires is that needed to manifest what one already is, the freedom of the acorn to grow into a full oak and not to be thwarted.

This gives an added point to his view of education as permissive and protecting, an idea derived from Rousseau who was anxious above all to prevent the child being corrupted by 'society' and 'words'. But in Froebel this negative education has a more positive purpose: to allow the divine spirit within the child to manifest itself. The divine action 'cannot be other than good if left undisturbed' and the child 'positively seeks that which is best for himself though he may do so unconsciously in a form appropriate to his abilities and means'. And so any prescriptive education must impede and destroy that expression of the divine essence within him. Only if it has been unquestionably impaired may control and direction be exercised, in order to restore it. Froebel can think of only two arguments for directive education: to teach 'the true self-evident idea' or 'the established and accepted ideal'. But the former derives its authority from the 'eternal principle' which demands spontaneity and self-determination in men who are created for freedom in God's image, and the latter, seen in the life of Christ, also came from God. And so human beings cannot be *formal* models for each other, since the perfect life is one of freely advancing 'according to the eternal law by...[one's] own determination and...own choice' [11].

We note in this account of man, the world and education, a combination of Christian Theism, Romantic expressionism and the idea of man as self-determining. Despite the appearance of some of the language in these and other passages, Froebel was no pantheist, and he expressly denied that God is embodied in the world and that Nature is God's body [12]. But as against the mechanistic universe of the new cosmology, continued in Deism, Froebel takes over the Romantic view of Nature as a living an organic unity, and of man as a part of it, ideas familiar to us in the early poetry of Wordsworth. But he does not reduce God to a spirit wholly within Nature,

20

though he emphasises God's activity within it. Yet, unlike the orthodox statements of Christian belief, Froebel has little awareness of original sin and sees the child, not as following the Way set out for him, which he needs to be taught, but as spontaneously expressing God's spirit within him. The child already *is* what he is to become. There is little or nothing of the death of the old man and the putting on of the new, of discipleship and discipline, nor of the duty of parents and teachers to train him in the way that he is to follow. Neither is there anything about existential choice, for, though the child is self-determining and not determined by others, he is so in the sense, not of an autonomous chooser and self-legislator as in Kant and our contemporary theory, but of a self *already formed* which needs only freely and without hindrance to express itself.

Froebel, of course, could not keep up the idea of the child as wholly unfolding from within. And he explicitly stated the need for a radical change of direction at the age of eight, when, instead of making the inward outer, the child is to make the outward inner, that is, to assimilate the world around him. Then education does become directive and actively teaches the child, as through the 'gifts', to recognise the unity of Nature and of himself with it [13].

Froebel's conception of education is therefore ultimately Reality-centred, centred upon God and Nature as God's creation, and not upon the isolated self of the child. But when there is lost the cosmological background to the idea of self-determination as self-expression, and thence to the task of education being to allow or to assist but never to direct that self-expression, what remains is the later child-centred notion of education, wherein also the child is taken to be already formed and not in the making and so not to need instruction and direction, which could only distort him. But that notion was one of mere *self*-expression, not expression of a divine spirit within the the self and then of coming to apprehend the unity of the world, oneself with it, and the dependence of both on God. Hence it was even less concerned than Froebel with the social and cultural world around the child, and not at all with the nature of the cosmos. I have not been able to trace any documented links between the later idea of self-expression and Froebel, but there is definitely this logical connection. Nor have I found any exposition of the idea of self-expression. It is a phrase which appears only as invoked and never argued for nor explained [14]. But we can see that it presupposes an anthropology of men as radically individual but already made, and thus with nothing to learn, and needing only the means of expression, curiously limited to verbal and visual arts, which education will provide. And it presupposes an acosmic cosmology: that is, the child is unsituated in a world, since there is nothing for him to learn about it, not so much self-defining man in a meaningless world as man already defined (by what?) in no world at all. Nevertheless, in its apparent acosmism and its implied anthropology, the idea of self-expression rejects any notion a a Law or Way which defines humanity, which we are to follow, and which we are to teach to the young for them to follow also. It therefore falls mostly within the distinctively modern cosmology.

Notes

1. See 'On Eternal Peace' in *Kant on History*.
2. *Critique of Pure Reason*, B xvi-xvii. The following references in the text are to the paragraphs of the *Prolegomena*.
3. See also, *Critique of Pure Reason*, A828-9, B856-7.
4. See also, on freedom, *Groundwork of the Metaphysics of Morals* (trans. as *The Moral Law*), pp. 1Ø7-2Ø.
5. See below, p.28, for Hegel's criticism.
6. Max Scheler, *Formalism in Ethics*, pp.11-23.
7. This leads Kant's to some forced arguments when, in his *Metaphysics of Morals*, he elaborates the whole duty of man: e.g. that in favour of monogamy, wherein

he states that in sexual relations one turns oneself into a thing, which is legitimate only if mutual and if one does not change partners. But that would legitimate any mutal agreement or render illegitimate the use of first one person and then another to do a job for oneself.

8. As in his *Religion within the Bounds of Pure Reason Alone.*
9. See C. Taylor, op.cit., pp.11–28.
1Ø. *Froebel: A Selection from His Writings*, pp.48–5Ø.
11. ibid. pp.51–4.
12. ibid. p.144.
13. See Bantock, *Studies*, II, pp.82–6, on the conflict between the endogenous and the exogenous aspects in Froebel's account of education.
14. As in D.H. Lawrence's 'Education of the People' (in *Phoenix*) of 1919, wherein the idea of education as self–expression is taken as familiar and as agreed.

4 Hegel: The self-definition of *Geist*

Hegel's is the most ambitious, comprehensive and systematic of all philosophies, and, because of its terminology, over-riding of ordinary logic, and complex inter-connections of any one aspect with every other, it defies summary. I, for one, find many passages nearly unintelligible without another's commentary. Yet it has a central and profound relevance to our theme, and includes a treatment of education, so that it is impossible to pass him by.

Hegel sought to synthesize the oppositions of his age, and, in relation to our theme, to combine the new emphasis upon human freedom and autonomy with the Romantic attempt to restore meaning to the universe by seeing it as an expression of spirit, mind or God. Hence the turn to Idealism, to interpreting the world as a projection of the Ego (Fichte) and Nature as 'petrified mind' (Schelling). This was an attempt to re-unite body and mind, the self and the world, sundered by Descartes and kept apart by Kant, not by reducing mind and the human world to mechanical Nature, but by raising the latter to the former. Hegel therefore interpreted the world, natural and human, as the rational and necessary self-development and self-expression of *Geist*, 'mind' or 'spirit', of which man is the self-conscious embodiment. This *Geist* is wholly immanent within the world, and hence Hegel's system is Pantheist rather than Theist, although he always maintained that he was a Lutheran and that his philosophy gave, in scientific form, the truth of Christianity. And onto this immanent Spirit Hegel relocated the task of self-definition in radical freedom, so as to restore meaning to the world and to human life but without returning to the older type of cosmology. It is not men who have to define themselves in the absence of a superior Law or Way, but *Geist* which defines itself and comes to know itself through the process of human history.

Furthermore, Hegel's system is the supreme expression of modern Gnosticism, and that in two ways. Firstly, *Geist*, in order to know itself and thus really to be itself, must project an alien world – that of inert Nature – into which it projects itself as the separate spirits which are human beings. It needs, as it were, a mirror which is not itself in order to see itself. What each of us really is, therefore, as in the Gnostic systems of old, is a fragment of *Geist* which, to begin with, does not know whence it has come or whither it is going. At the present time (i.e. of Hegel himself), it has dawned on many that we are faced with an alien world, in Nature and in our *milieux*. The former is a dead mechanism, and the latter something which the individual knows he has not created and which would define him from the outside. This latter alienation, which we have seen in Rousseau, issues in a desire for absolute freedom, a freedom from all constraints and external influences. But this, as the French Revolution proved, is self-destructive (*PR* 5R, 29R, 258R; *PG* 582–95) [1]. For it is a desire which refuses to be tied down to anything definite, to be one thing and therefore not another, but vainly seeks (as we saw in Rousseau) to realise the abstract universal: for example, to be a man with being tied down to being a Frenchman or a German. This desire can therefore satisfy itself only by destruction, by tearing down barriers to a freedom which cannot exist because it is purely abstract. But whereas ancient Gnosticism sought an escape from this world, Hegel seeks to reconcile men to it. He therefore seeks to show that the very otherness of Nature from man is in reality a token of its kinship. For it also is a projection of Spirit and is needed by for Spirit to realize itself. The modern view of Nature, presupposed by natural science, therefore is true, on one level. But, on a higher and philosophical level, Nature is seen to be an essential element within the life of Spirit after all. Likewise the social world rightly appears as alien to men who have reached the stage of individual self-consciousness and self-responsibility, wherein they stand on their individual rights and make contracts with each other. But, again, that is not the final truth but only a stage on the way to it. That way of viewing man and society, as we find it in Hobbes, Locke, Hume, the Utilitarians, Kant and one side of Rousseau, has to be 'overcome'. On a truly philosophical level, we see that the social world around us, which others have created and which is not the product of our own individual wills, is after all an expression of that Spirit of which we too are expressions. It lives in and through it as it does in and through each of us. And now (i.e. in the time of the birth of the modern state and of Hegel's philosophy) that Spirit is coming at last fully to realize itself in the human world and in men's minds. Hegel therefore claims to tell us whence we have come and whither we are going, not out of this world but to a consummation of Spirit's quest for itself within it. Again, the End is to be realized within this world and human history, not beyond them.

Secondly, as opposed to those Romantic philosophers who despised Reason, which they identified with the deadening analysis of natural science and who exalted intuition in its place, and also to religion which is based on Faith, Hegel claims to *know*, to know by Reason and Science, that the world is as he says it is. He takes over Kant's distinction between Understanding and Reason but refuses to have the latter limited, as Kant limited it, to merely pointing out that Understanding deals with phenomena and not the unknowable things-in-themselves. He rejects Kant's 'critical' approach on the grounds that it rests upon an uncriticized analogy of cognition as an instrument or passive medium, which Critical philosophy is to test by turning it upon itself. But, says Hegel, an instrument changes its object and a passive medium diffracts it, so that either way, and in criticizing itself, it will never give knowledge of things as they are, including itself as it is (*PG* 73–4). Kant erred in demanding that we know before we can know, that we do not enter the water until we can swim (*L* 41 R; cf 1∅) and his 'thing-in-itself' is merely negative, an 'utter abstraction' and 'total emptiness', and, far from being unknown, it is the easiest thing to know (*L* 44). Kant was wrong to take his phenomena as merely phenomena *for us*, and not as phenomena in their own nature and as founded not in themselves but in the 'universal divine Idea', so that, instead of Kant's subjective Idealism (which Kant himself called 'transcendental'), Hegel's philosophy is 'absolute Idealism' (*L* 45 R). The real meaning of Kant's Antimonies of Reason is not that Reason contradicts itself, but that contradictions exists in things: i.e. they are not self-

24

subsistent entities but 'moments' of a whole from which they cannot be separated (*L* 48 R). Hegel thereby clears the way for his confident and untrammelled use of Reason, which he calls 'Speculation' and 'Science'.

Philosophy, then, as Reason goes beyond the hard and fast and mutually exclusive categories of the Understanding, which Hegel also calls 'reflection' and holds to be appropriate to the empirical (but not speculative or philosophical) study of Nature and to characterize thinking in 'civil society' where men see themselves as atomic individuals joined by mutual contracts for common purposes. (It is the form of thinking typical of Empiricist and Analytic philosophy). In contrast, Hegel takes reality to be a self-differentiating and self-developing whole, containing difference within itself. It has three basic moments: as it is in itself, implicitly and 'immediately'; as it externalizes itself in Nature, a realm of otherness; and as it comes back to itself, to consciousness of itself, in human history. And every aspect of reality reflects this basic structure in one way or another. Philosophy therefore has three corresponding divisions: Logic, which studies the Idea in and for itself, the system of rational, necessary and self-differentiating categories; Philosophy of Nature which studies the traces of the Idea in Nature as its external embodiment; and Philosophy of Spirit which studies the ways in which through human knowledge, history, Art, Religion, Philosophy and finally Hegel's philosophy itself, the Idea comes to know itself with increasing and finally complete self-comprehension. Logic therefore coincides with metaphysics as '*the science of things set and held in thoughts* – thoughts accredited able to express the essential reality of things'. The other philosophical sciences are applied logic (*L* 24) [2].

Perhaps the easiest introduction to Hegel is his *Reason in History*, the Introduction to his *Lectures on World History*, where, with less of his complex dialectic, he expounds his conception of the world process, and especially of how Spirit, as World Spirit, differentiates itself into the Spirits which are the common minds of and which form the particular nations. Each in turn has a particular destiny and role to play in the self-realization of Spirit. God, the World Spirit is immanent within the world, each consciousness and world-history: 'If the divine being were not the essence of man and nature, it would in fact not be a being at all' (*RH* pp.52-3 – these pages give a very clear statement of Hegel's conceptions of world history, the spirit of a nation, and the individual, as the vehicles of Spirit which is wholly immanent within them).

We can now see how Hegel reconciled the modern anthropology of man as self-defining subject with a world which had become meaningless. In the section 'B. Self-Consciousness' of the *Phenomenology*, Hegel interprets man as having a fundamental desire to possess his world, to negate it in finding himself in and through it: what man as self-consciousness really seeks is himself (167). We cannot retrace here the dialectic which moves this search through the life-and-death struggle, lordship and bondage, Stoicism, Scepticism and the Unhappy Consciousness (some of the best known passages in Hegel), save only to point out that in Stoicism what emerges is the desire for autonomy and independence, epistemological and social, which continues in Scepticism and the Unhappy Consciousness, which projects its conception of what it really is and should be into a Beyond which it cannot attain. The upshot of this progress is that Spirit is now implicitly aware of itself as one with all reality (a wholly this-worldly reality, of course) (23∅). The rest of the *Phenomenology* shows how, through many turns of dialectic and 'shapes' of consciousness Spirit eventually becomes totally explicit. It is not the individual who defines himself, but Spirit, which dirempts itself into the world of Nature and human individuals. That world now regains meaning for man as, with himself, a 'moment' in the self-realization of Spirit.

The same interpretation is given more succinctly in *Reason in History* (p.48). The self that depends on something else is bound to it and by it. Therefore self-sufficiency brings freedom. Consequently, spirit (*Geist*) seeks to 'produce itself, to make itself its own object, and to gain knowledge of itself; in this way, it exists for itself'. But, of course, the single individual is not and can never be self-sufficient. And, to overcome (to cancel while preserving) this sense of dependence, Hegel interprets him as but an accident of the Spirit that is the one real substance, and which differentiates itself and thereby realizes itself in and through Nature, individuals, nations and world-history. That movement is traced in the Philosophies of Nature and Spirit. We shall now take it up in *The Philosophy of Right*, which will bring us to Hegel's treatment of education.

The aim of that work is to demonstrate the essential rationality of the state (*PR* p.11), i.e. the modern state emerging n Hegel's time which is based on the freedom of the individual. Now Hegel, although he may originally take his theses from history and political experience, would consider it unphilosophical to argue for them merely on that basis: indeed, it is for philosophy to show the inherent rationality and necessity of the main trends of history despite their contingent detail. Hence he seeks to deduce them, with dialectic, from 'the concept' (or 'notion'). So he begins with a summary of the conclusions of *The Philosophy of Mind* as to the nature of Will.

But, first of all, let us note that Hegel is no Legal Positivist and does not lose the question of the rationality of a law in that of whether or not it has been enacted and is enforced. A law may be valid but that does not make it rational, and Hegel gives examples of valid yet irrational laws from Roman law (*PR* 3 & R). But, in contrast to traditional cosmologies, Hegel does not seek the standard for human laws in a transcendent Law or Way. Although his *Philosophy of Right* is also titled *Natural Law and Political Science in Outline*, it seeks the rightness of law within the rational will, not the private will of the individual, but the will that is an essential moment in the self-development of Spirit as freedom. Thus it is a wholly immanent standard, defined by Spirit which gives it as a law to itself, and thus to men and states as its vehicles. In this way he sought to overcome the emptiness and abstractness of Kant's Categorical Imperative, it too founded upon the rational will but upon the rational will as only an abstract idea and not as a moment of the self-determining Spirit which produces the universe as its self-determination and self-expression.

The basis of right (*Recht* = *ius*, for which there is no single English equivalent, and which is to be taken as referring to personal duties and rights as well as to communal laws and the administration of justice) is mind (spirit), specifically the will which is essentially free. Freedom is therefore 'the substance of right and its goal, while the system of right is the realm of freedom made actual, the world of mind [spirit] brought forth out of itself like a second nature' (*PR* 4). That is, freedom is specified in terms of right; what is right, is what is necessary for freedom to exist; and right is embodied in the human world which spirit (essentially freedom) has created as its self-expression. Will has three 'moments': (a) that of 'pure indeterminacy', the ability to dissipate, to say 'no' to, whatever desires and impulses arise in oneself (*PR* 5); (b) the 'transition from undifferentiated indeterminancy to the differentiation, determination and positing of a determinacy as a content and object', the ability to move from the hovering over oneself that is (a) to willing something in particular. But, in Hegel's logic, (b) is already but implicitly contained in (a), which by itself is, or is an example of, false infinity and not the true infinity which specifies itself in its finite details (*PR*6 & R). For willing is not pure willing, which would be the willing of nothing, but the willing of something, and to be a will the will must restrict itself in something finite (*PR* 6 A). The third moment (c) is the unity of (a) and (b), 'the *self*-determination of the ego', the ego positing itself simultaneously as restricted and determinate (that which is willed) and as itself, above and not constrained by that which it wills and into which it puts itself. Thus it is 'the innermost secret of speculation' (i.e. of Hegel's philosophy), 'infinity as negativity relating itself to itself, this ultimate spring of all activity, life and consciousness' – the power of self-differentiation which is Spirit and the basis of the world-process (*PR* 7 & R). This is how he overcomes that resentment of differentiation of roles and of having to be something in particular which we saw in Rousseau and shall see also in Marx, and which is to be found in other forms today, such as Feminism.

In *PR* 11–18 Hegel's describes the natural will or impulses and desires, which is implicitly free but which does not yet have itself as its object. In 19 onwards Hegel develops the genuine form of the will from the rationalizing of desires and impulses. 'A will is truly a will only when what it wills, its content, is identical with itself, when that is to say, freedom wills freedom' (*PR* 21 A, p.232). This means that what seems external to it – the customs, laws and institutions of the state – is in fact itself, for the will embodies itself in them (*PR* 22 & Knox's note p.317). The absolute goal of free mind is to make freedom its object and to embody freedom in actual fact, the human world around us (*PR* 27). Right is thus 'an existent of any sort embodying the free will' (*PR* 29). Here we have the keystone of Hegel's moral and social philosophy: on the one side, Spirit as freedom is its own end and so the source of duty and law and rights for the individual and in the state; on the other, the free will, the proximate source of duty law and right, is not confined to the free will of the individual but is to be found also in custom, positive law, institutions and all aspects of the human world, since those and the individual are moments in the self-development of Spirit. Right is sacrosanct only as the embodiment of self-conscious freedom – freedom as aware of itself and making itself its goal (*PR* 3∅).

The absolutely free will has three stages of development: A. 'immediate' and abstract, the rights of the person and as person and thus of his property in which he embodies and through which he expresses and executes his will – Abstract or Formal Right; B. the right of the inner person, of his subjective will and conscience determing the good for himself – the sphere of Morality (*Moralität*); and C. the unity of the abstractly separated moments A and B, the good as existing both in the individual will and in external world, the sphere of Ethical Life (*Sittlichkeit*). This last, on the same principle, is also divided into: (a) a natural stage – the Family; (b) a stage of separation and division – Civil Society; and (c) 'the State as freedom, freedom universal and objective even in the free self-subsistence of the particular will', which appears first as the 'actual and organic mind' of a single nation, then in inter-relation of particular national minds, and then in 'the universal world-mind whose right is supreme' (*PR* 33).

We have considered the foregoing, the Introduction to *PR*, in some detail because it clearly shows how Hegel derives from Spirit as freedom the whole duty of man and state (including family and other associations), and how he seeks to make it concrete by giving it a definite content, but one out of itself, not something alien from the outside. In this way he seeks to overcome the paralysis or destructiveness which otherwise comes from the desire for radical freedom – to make oneself throughout, to depend upon nothing external, to be completely autonomous. As we have seen, Hegel agrees that radical freedom is what freedom is. But when the subjective will or merely private and single individual, or a collection of such, aspires to attain such freedom, then either (a) the will is paralysed in having nothing by which to choose, since it is the empty nothingness of 'I = I' and the indeterminancy which floats above desires and impulses and cannot now realise itself in anything in particular, or (b) it resents all concrete existence as imposing limits, and refusing to be a 'somewhat' or something in particular and thus *not* other things (what economists call 'opportunity cost'), and so seeks to tear them down in a fury of destructiveness for its own sake. The former we shall find in Sartre's Existentialism, in which man being doomed to freedom and having no values to guide him, can act only in 'bad faith' or attempt to express his radical freedom in an irrational and unmotivated *acte gratuite*. The latter Hegel rightly saw in the Terror of the French Revolution.

Freedom is, then, to be found first in the inferior sphere of abstract individuals and their property rights, which are fundamentally negative – rights not to be interfered with and duties of others to keep their hands off. That passes over into the intermediate sphere of Morality, the morality of the individual guided by his conscience. Here Hegel takes advantage of the connection between *Gewissen*, 'conscience', and *Gewißheit*, 'certainty', to interpret conscience as certainty of good and duty. He thus rules out the possibility of a hesitant conscience, one perplexed and then resolving upon a line of duty but ready to admit that it may be wrong. Thus Hegel generates a slide from conscience as consciousness of good and duty to conscience as *making up*, in subjective self-certainty, goood and duty, and thus lapsing into a self-contradictory subjectivism (*PR* 137 & R). He also interprets Kant's ethics as those of Morality and not Ethical Life, and rightly points out that Kant's Categorical Imperative, in being purely formal, is thereby purely negative and requires good and duty to be only self-consistent. It can therefore endorse any content, and Kant has simply to assume, for example, that property and human life are to exist and be respected. But the absence of property is as consistent as its existence, and likewise human life, and so theft and murder are not inherently self-contradictory nor, on Kant's principles, are they inherently immoral (*PR* 135R). These self-contradictions cause Morality to pass over into Ethical Life or concrete ethics. But, it is important to note, the abstract rights of the person and the rights of conscience, are preserved while their contradictions and limitations are overcome in Ethical Life. And so the final account of the State is of the modern State of freedom with representative institutions and the rule of law emerging in Hegel's own day (and *not* actualized in Prussia) – an internally diversified State, socially with classes, families and corporations, and constitutionally with 'Estates', monarchy, courts and civil service (all, of course, deduced from 'the concept' and thereby shown to be rationally necessary and historically inevitable), and not the blank, undifferentiated, unlimited and thus totalitarian democracy of Rousseau and (after Hegel) Marx.

We can now pass to the bearings upon education of his general philosophy. Firstly something that, so far as I know, remains implicit in his writings: the futility of any abstract specification of the content of education, such as whether or not 'the educated man' is to know or not the constitution of Peru [3]. One can be educated in only what the progress of Spirit has so far created out of itself and for itself: one cannot be taught what has not yet happened or been discovered or invented, e.g. the constitution of Peru before Peru existed and before it had a constitution. Again, Hegel's emphasis upon the diremption of Spirit into the particular spirits of the particular nations entails, I think, that education is appropriately confined to what one's own national Spirit has so far created in its progress: that one should be taught the constitution of Peru only if one is a Peruvian. One would take this to be simple common sense, that the young learn what will shape their lives in their respective *milieux*. This, let us note, does not entail restriction to what is contemporary, for historical development is cumulative, and some nations clearly encapsulate a distinct past, as European civilization encapsulates Greek and Roman civilization and the religious legacy of Israel, which for centuries constituted the main content of its formal education. What Hegel would reject, and would be committed to rejecting, so it appears to me, is, on the one hand, a merely abstract account of a curriculum supposedly universally applicable, and, on the other, the incorporation of extraneous elements into a curriculum, such as teaching Swahili in Europe or Chinese in Africa (that is, generally and not just to a specialist few for specific purposes, such as business, diplomacy and scholarship). His emphasis upon Ethical Life, embedded in specific customs, institutions and laws, requires an organic unity among its elements, not a discordant intrusion of alien elements.

This takes us to the question of historical relativism often raised in relation to Hegel: viz. that he denies any universal and trans-historical moral laws and leaves us only with those of our nation and age. As we have seen, this is not true and he has a universal principle of freedom. But what he would insist upon is that one cannot be obliged by duties which the Spirit in its progress has not yet developed out of itself. Thus, he thought, the Greeks had not yet recognised the fact and rights of conscience, though it was struggling for recognition in the Sophists and Socrates, but it had to wait for Christianity to become 'actual' – realized and recognized in fact (Knox's notes to PR 14∅, 151, pp.343, 351). If he was right in this, then one cannot blame the Greeks for taking conformity with customary morality to be sufficient, just as one cannot blame them for not having a planetary conception of the atom. Either would be sheer anachronism. Hence the insistence upon Ethical Life, upon actual laws, rights and institutions, and hence upon the need for education to immerse the young in them, does not entail relativism. What else can people do, except to have and to impart no morality at all? It is exactly the same as teaching the mother-tongue: what other language can one teach at the start? And in quoting the Greek commonplace, that the best way of educating a child is to 'make him a citizen of state with good laws' (PR 153R), we note that it is not any state which is recommended (and 'laws' here has its Greek meaning of customary morality, personal and public, as well as what we call 'laws').

What can, and should, be urged against Hegel, is that he does not recognize, and his whole philosophy of immanent and self-developing Spirit prevents him from recognizing, any universal standards open to all, a Natural Law or Tao which all can and do recognize, though parts of it become obscured or restricted by individuals and peoples [4]. But Hegel holds that Spirit starts in 'immediacy', as merely 'implicit', just as child is only immediately and implicitly an adult, and history is its path to self-discovery through self-creation. Hence, in his view, the fundamentals of morality emerge successively in history as part of that path to self-discovery, and so it is only now, in the Christian world and specifically in the emerging state of the 'Germanic' realm – northern Europe and North America – (PR 358), that the full and genuine moral law of freedom is being recognized and turned into fact.

But what of times, like our own, where there is not the solid body of customary law, right, duty and institutions (Sitten) to which Hegel refers? Well, they are times of transition, as the cosmopolitan Roman Empire was, between the decay of the ancient world, Greek and Roman, and the birth of the new Christian Europe. In such a time, it is inevitable that the outer world will seem alien; that men will turn in upon themselves; that philosophies like Scepticism and Stoicism (which invented the word and idea of 'cosmopolis') will prevail; and that Moralität will replace a faded Sittlichkeit (cf PG 199). But such, for Hegel, are not happy times, though necessary stages in the self-development of Spirit. And they certainly are not normative: they add something in their negative attitude to the outer world and development of subjectivity; but that is to be overcome in a new and higher unity of inner and outer, subjectivity and objectivity. Inevitably, education in such a time will be polyglot, individualistic and only abstractly universal (cosmopolitan), since there is little actual Ethical Life or shared understanding of man and his duty embodied in concrete institutions and customs. Were Hegel with us today, he might be tempted to see this new turn away from solid tradition to individualism as a necessary stage leading, along with its mirror-opposite in the recently departed totalitarian states, to a truly universal world-order of concrete freedom.

But we should return to what Hegel actually wrote. As we would expect, he repudiates the isolation of the child advocated by Rousseau in Émile. He comments that attempts at this have proved futile 'since no success can attend an attempt to estrange people from the laws of the world' and the world mind will reach to any outlying region where such isolation might be attempted (PR 153A, p.261). For education is 'the art of making men ethical' (conscientious performers of objective duties), begins with the child at the level of instinct and shows him the way to 'a second birth', to a 'second, intellectual, nature', which it makes habitual (PR 151 A, p.26∅). That is, it inducts children into the actual world around them of customary roles, duties, rights, laws and institutions, wherein they attain the genuinely human

29

and adult level of existence. It is their right to be brought to freedom and thus (as we have seen) to belong to 'an actual ethical order, because their conviction of their freedom finds its truth [fulfilment] in such an objective order' (*PR* 153). Of course, many an actual ethical order is deficient in, or even devoid of freedom, whether or not those within it realize this or not. But, Hegel would insist, it is futile, à la Rousseau, to bring up the young outside society and the world of 'objective mind', Spirit made actual in the human world. Reflection, the activity of Understanding, estimates and compares impulses and so gives them 'abstract universality', and it is this 'growth of the universality of thought' which is the 'absolute value in education' (*PR* 58). Hence Hegel criticizes both Romantic primitivism, the desire to return to a simpler and supposedly more natural state, and treating the particularity of people – their merely subjective desires – as an absolute end. For the former treats education (*Bildung* – a term with a wide meaning more like 'formation') as external and an 'ally of corruption', and the latter as something merely instrumental to those private ends, pleasure for pleasure's sake. But mind essentially aims at overcoming a merely natural state, thus first at developing Understanding and thinking in terms of universals, in which its 'freedom is existent and mind becomes objective to itself', and then beyond that to a concrete union of universality and particularity in the individual person freely realising himself in the ethical order of his state. Therefore aims at 'liberation and the struggle for higher liberation still'. It is the 'absolute transition from an ethical substantiality which is immediate and natural to the one which is intellectual and so both infinitely subjective and lofty enough to have attained universality of form'. For the individual, this is a difficult process, a struggle against impulse, caprice and pre-occupation with one's merely subjective self. (Hegel would reject any attempt to make education painless – cf *PG* 19 on 'the seriousness, the suffering, the patience, and the labour of the negative'.) From the attainment of universality in the Understanding, the particular person then becomes the union of universality and particularity – the genuine individual, 'infinitely independent free subjectivity'. This is 'the position which reveals education as a moment immanent in the Absolute and which makes plain its infinite value' (*PR* 187 R – and 187 A, p.268 on education as rubbing off rough edges). That is, only through education, which here, I think, means specifically an intellectual education and thus the development of abstract forms of thought, can Spirit attain its ultimate end of attaining knowledge of itself as the freedom and subject that it is.

So much, then, for the chief tasks and real significance of education. We shall now follow Hegel's treatment of education in the contexts of the family, civil society and the state. (It is noteworthy that it is not mentioned in the First and Second Parts, on Abstract Right and Morality, respectively, for there Hegel treats of essentially particular and private moments or stages, and education is essentially a matter of one person taking responsibility for the development of another.) Throughout, Hegel treats the family, civil society and the state in terms of 'the concept', that is, as embodiments of freedom and thus in the form which they have now attained. Hence he affirms the child's right to maintenance and education at the expense of the common capital of the family, and the the limitation of parents' rights over them and their wishes – to what is required for discipline and education (*PR* 174). As potential freedom, children are not things and so not the property of their parents (as they were in Roman law which Hegel castigates on this point). Within the family, the task of education is to instill into the child ethical principles 'in the form of immediate feeling' so that 'his heart may live its early years in love, trust, and obedience'. It therein has the task of raising the child out of the instinctive level to freedom of personality and self-subsistence, wherein he can leave the family (which did not happen in patriarchical society, where all were members of one family and nothing more) (*PR* 175). But Hegel is rightly opposed to child-centred notions of education, which would lock the child in his subjective self. Discipline is needed within education 'to break the child's self-will and thereby eradicate his purely natural and sensuous self'. This cannot be done by mere goodness, for in their immediate state children act by fancies and caprices. Likewise he rightly rejects the modern method of substituting reasons for discipline, because it leaves it open to children 'to decide whether the reasons are weighty or not, and thus we make everything depend on their whim'. As far children are concerned, 'universality and the substance of things' reside in parents, so that children must be obedient. 'If the feeling of subordination, producing the longing to grow up, is not fostered in children, they become forward and impertinent' (*PR* 174 A, p.265). The point is that child-centred approaches would not induce the ability and habit of thinking and ruling themselves in terms of universal conceptions, despite the pretence of doing so in reasoning with them. Hegel has a far better insight into the child's mind than the progressives in education. He rightly sees the he necessity for education as present in children 'as their own feeling of dissatisfaction with themselves as they are, as the desire to belong to the adult world whose superiority they divine, as the longing to grow up'. The play theory of education 'assumes that what is childish is itself already something of inherent worth and presents it as such to the children'. It thus makes education and its contents a form of childishness which children themselves do not respect. It makes out childish immaturity to be maturity, and would have children satisfied with themselves as they are. And so it corrupts children, destroys their proper desire for something better, and induces in them vanity and conceit (*PR* 175 R).

The sphere of Civil Society is the realm of the Understanding, men as self-subsistent individuals joined by contract in associations for mutual benefit and purposes – the world of business, commerce, arts and sciences (and Empiricist and Analytical Philosophy). Thus it provides a training of the intellect at this level, flexibility of mind and thinking in terms of general relations. And practical education – the mastery of any craft or trade – produces from its discipline of adapting oneself to materials and the pleasure of other workers (and customers, we may add) a habit 'of objective activity and universally recognized aptitudes' (*PR* 197). Law and the courts also belong to Civil Society, where they are seen as institutions established to further mutual interests. Here abstract right – to oneself and one's property – is universally recognized and made objective in a body of law and its administration. This also educates men to think in terms of relations, and thus to see themselves as instances of universals, the universal of humanity as such, and to realize that they count as men in virtue of this and not because of their particular nationality, race, religion or other denomination (*PR* 2Ø9 & R) [5]. The commercial, industrial and professional side of Civil Society is, or ought to be, organized into Corporations (like the Law Society), which look after their own interests, co-opt new members from those qualified by skill and rectitude, protect their members against particular contigencies, and provide schemes of education to fit others to become members (*PR* 252). Hegel, it seems, would thus confine technical and profession education to Corporations. He does not envisage qualification and certification outside of membership of such a body nor teaching by wholly independent institutions such as Colleges of FE and Polytechnics. This is because he stresses the internal differentiation of the state, and thus all the institutions intermediary between the forms of government and the single individual, and thinks that the social classes should be represented as such in Parliament – hence 'Estate' is used in the translation to refer to the chambers of Parliament. In contrast, both the Individualist social philosophy of Empiricism (especially that of Hobbes and the Utilitarians) and the totalitarian democracy of Rousseau, the Jacobins and Marx and his followers, dissolve all such intermediary bodies – the former in theory by making men mere atoms and the latter in practice by repression, while the Corporativist form of totalitarianism, as with Mussolini and Gentile (in theory), forcibly organises individuals into Corporations, allows them no individual rights, and has the

Corporations constitute the organs of government but under the control of the Party.

Curiously, little is said of education in relation to the sphere of the State, only that the opening of the Estates–Assemblies (the Chambers of Parliament) to the public is a means, a chief means, of the education of adult individuals (*PR* 315), and that an education is needed which will make possible the foundation of the state upon the free assent and willing activity of its citizens (*PR* 270). Here remains much for others to do: to see how far can be 'deduced from the concept' a determinate curriculum for education in the modern state; specific institutions, schools and colleges and others, wherein it would be taught; their internal organisation; their ownership and relation to the government; and teachers as a distinct Corporation. It is not a task which I shall attempt, but it would be very interesting to see attempts at the completion of a Hegelian philosophy of education.

We leave Hegel by noting how he deduced a traditional view of education, or the elements of one, from his own version of the new cosmology and anthropology. The decisive different is that self–definition is displaced from the particular and subjective self and onto Spirit which defines and realizes itself in the world, natural and human, and is thus to be found on both the inner and external worlds. Hence by assimilating one's *milieu* and adapting oneself to it, above all in the modern state of freedom now coming into birth, one realizes one's own subjective freedom and therein Spirit is attaining its self–realization and self–knowledge. Man is thus reconciled to the world and to his place in it, and to the education needed for fulfilment of himself in that place. Yet, despite the use of the language of Christian Theism, there is no use of the substance of Theism or any other traditional cosmology. Man is not under a transcendent Law or Way; and duty, right and the social order flow from the rational will which is the freedom of Spirit realising itself wholly from itself. We now turn to Marx's rewriting of Hegel, wherein also there is no Law or Way presented by or through the world and it is not really the particular subject who defines himself.

Notes

1. References to Hegel's works will be by means of the following abbreviations:
   L   =   Logic, the 'Shorter Logic', the first part of *The Encyclopaedia of the Philosophical Sciences*;
   PG   = *Phenomenology of Spirit*;
   PR   = *Philosophy of Right*;
   RH   = *Reason in History*, the Introduction to *The Lectures on World History*. Also R = 'Remark', the notes added by Hegel to the paragraphs of *L* and *PR*, and A = 'Addition', by the editors, of material from Hegel's lectures. Thus '10R' and '11A' refer, respectively, to the Remark added to 10 and the Addition to 11, while '12 & R' refers to 12 and the Remark added to it.
2. *The Philosophy of Nature* and *The Philosophy of Spirit (Mind)* are, respectively, the second and third parts of *The Encyclopaedia*, while *PG* leads up to it, and *PR* and the lectures on Aesthetics, History of Philosophy, Philosophy of Religion, and World History are extensions of *The Philosophy of Spirit*.
3. A question solemnly discussed by Downie, Loudfoot and Telfer in their *Education and Personal Relations*.
4. Hegel quotes the *Antigone* on 'the unwritten laws' (*PR* 166R; *PG* 437) but confines them to family law and piety, the sphere of the woman in the home.
5. Note here how, contrary to some accounts, Hegel affirms rights pertaining to humanity as such.

5 Marx: Towards socialist man

Marx explicitly stated that metaphysics, with morality and religion, has no independent existence and history, and that philosophy ends where genuine science begins [1]. But Marx has his own metaphysics and philosophical account of man, which is implicitly exempted from the merely epiphenomenal character ascribed to other systems. Let us now see what that was.

Marx openly avowed himself to be a follower of Hegel, whose dialectic, he claimed, stood on its head and so suffered from mystification. Marx claimed to have turned it the right way up and thus to have freed its rational core [2]. Philosophy, he wrote, begins with the confession of Aeschylus' Prometheus: 'In a word, I hate all gods' [3]. His social criticism took over and continued the religious criticism of Feuerbach, which held religion to be the creation of man. Feeling himself to be unreal, man has projected a superman in the heavens. But the suffering, of which religion is the expression, is real, so that 'Religion is the sigh of the oppressed creature, the feeling of a heartless world, and the soul of soulless circumstances. It is the opium of the people'. The illusory happiness offered by religion is to be replaced by genuine happiness [4]. This rejection of religion is, in effect, a rejection of any notion of a Law or Way above and beyond man, so that we have in Marx another variation on the theme of man as a self-defining subject. But Marx does not simply revert to that idea after Hegel had attempted to redefine it and to restore meaning to the world. For while he eliminated Hegel's cosmic Spirit, and, instead, made man the determiner of his destiny, he continued to use much of Hegel's terminology, ideas and style of arguing (assertions of identity among highly abstract conceptions with no empirical reference and evidence). And so, as well as denying that 'history' does anything and affirming that events are the results of the actions of actual men [5], he did not hold mankind to be simply a mass of individuals each of whom has to define himself and to work out his own path in this life, but he saw mankind as in some way a corporate entity engaged in a collective enterprise and destiny. Therefore, while nothing over and above man, not even an Hegelian Spirit which is wholly immanent in the world, sets mankind a Way and defines what it is to be human,

33

nevertheless it is more mankind as a whole that works out one way and definition for itself in this, the only, world.

What Marx offers us is still a Gnostic drama: man was in a primal state of happiness ('primitive communism'); then he fell into one of 'alienation' and lack of freedom, of which the root causes are private property and the division of labour, and which gets progressively worse in contemporary industrial society; from that he will be delivered by a transforming Revolution into first a state of Communism, where private property will be abolished, and then into one of genuine Socialism, in which he will experience freedom along with the genuine benefits of industry, for then the economy will be consciously planned by everyone. The alienation of individuals from each other will thereby be overcome, as well as that of the individual from himself. (We note the similarity to Rousseau's yearning for a total democracy wherein everything will proceed from the will of each in union with the wills of everyone else.) Marxism is itself the *gnosis*, the knowledge, of whence we have come, of where we are and the evils of our present state, and of whither we can escape. And one distinctive element in this drama is the central importance given to labour, production and economic activity and conditions.

We shall now briefly review some of the main themes in Marx's account of man and the world as found in two of his 'Economic and Philosophical Manuscripts' 'Alienated Labour' and 'Private Property and Communism' [6].

Although it is central to Marx's criticism of contemporary society, his idea of the 'alienation' of labour is by no means clear. Fortunately, for our purposes we can pass over much of it, and concentrate on Marx's positive notion of man as realising himself in work. 'Alienation' in work means, among other things, that the worker has little control over his work and so does not realise himself in his work, not merely that he is poorly paid for it. His labour 'is not the satisfaction of a need but only a means to satisfy needs outside itself', as shown by his avoidance of it when there is no compulsion to work. And so the worker feels free only when not working and therefore only when 'eating, drinking and procreating, at most also in his dwelling and dress' (pp.8Ø–81). What is implied here is that the essential activity of man is work, producing things, and that, in Marx's view, the current nature of work is a perversion of that activity and of man's essence. Marx was greatly impressed by Hegel's treatment of master and slave (lord and bondsman) in the *Phenomenology* (195), especially the point at which Hegel asserts that, after all, the slave has the higher self-consciousness in and through his work which makes something relatively permanent and independent in which the worker sees his own independence. Marx took this up and saw men as making and affirming themselves in and through work, the transformation of Nature.

Man is a worker, but men are not merely individual workers, nor yet only workers in intimate relations with each other, but in some way appear to form a collective or corporate entity. Marx refers to mankind as a 'species-being', by which he appears to mean: (a) that there is a common human nature shared by all men; (b) that men are aware of this nature which they share, and of each other as belonging to human race, and so they can and do act in relation to each other and the whole species, even when not obviously doing so (cf. p.9Ø); and (c) that somehow the human race acts as a single entity. Or, rather, since Marx uses a compacted and undifferentiated terminology, and fails to give concrete evidence and examples, it is never clear which of these possible meanings of 'man' is intended and which not intended. Thus, it appears, that meaning (c) must be included in the statement that the whole of nature is man's organic body, for it is his means of subsistence and the material object and tool of his activity (p.81). Yet no one man nor any local group can make the *whole* of nature into his or its inorganic body, and even mankind as a corporate body is confined to the Earth.

'Alienated labour' is said to make man's species-character, that activity of free and conscious production which distinguishes men from the immediate production practised by animals, into a mere means for the individual's own physical existence presumably, individuals see their human powers only as useful in earning a living. But because of the way Marx expresses this (the compacted meaning of 'species-being', 'species-life', as meaning both 'human essence' and 'human race'), it asserts also that men also see the rest of the human race as a mere means to their own existence and thus they are alienated from it and from their own human nature. In contrast to animals which produce (reproduce) only themselves, 'men produce freely and not just from physical need, and only truly produce when they freely produce', and reproduce the rest of Nature in works of art. Marx concludes that it is transforming the natural world that man first really affirms himself as a species-being. 'This production is his active species-life. Through it nature appears as his work and his reality'. And so alienated labour tears man from himself, his human essence, the human race and the rest of nature (p.82).

Alienated labour, as the cause of these other ills, is itself the effect of private property and the division of labour. Yet these are necessary steps on the way to the final consumation of the human drama in state of socialism. (We note Marx's continuation of the Hegelian style of theodicy but with attention focused on the ills of the present and the eschatological promise.) Communism not the 'crude communism' of envious levelling down which is still dominated by the idea of private property which it merely generalises (pp.87-8) (i.e. what Socialist and Communist parties in fact practise) is the complete regaining by man of his essential nature and conserves everything that has been achieved in the course of history, the overcoming of the conflicts between man and nature, man and man, between existence and essence, objectification by others and self-affirmation (we shall hear more of this when we come to Sartre), freedom and necessity, and the individual and the species. 'It is the solution to the riddle of history and knows itself to be this solution' (p.89). How this supposed to come about, and whether the projected ideal is coherent, do not concern us now, only the fact that for Marx this is the ideal existence for man and his future destiny. Perhaps because he was too pre-occupied with present evils, perhaps because he suspected that this ideal might be incoherent, perhaps because any attempt concretely to picture complete felicity falls into banality and would seem tame recompense for the enormity (as it appeared to Marx) of human suffering in the meantime, or for other reasons, Marx gave little positive indication of what the end state of the drama would be. In *The German Ideology* he stated that the division of labour forces man into an exclusive sphere of activity, from which he cannot escape unless he wishes to lose his livelihood. But when 'society' (who? how?) regulates production, it will be possible for me 'to do one thing today and another tomorrow, to hunt in the morning, fish in the afternoon, rear cattle in the evening, criticize after dinner' but without ever becoming 'hunter, fisherman, cowherd or critic' (p.169). But Marx wished to have such a life *with* modern industry, yet to reduce the realm of necessity, those things which men *have* to do to meet external needs, while not eliminating it, so that the 'realm of freedom', of producing for its own sake, may increase [7]. Marx was no William Morris who wished to abolish industrial production, yet he simply ignored the organizational exigiences of large-scale industry, the fact that some must direct and manage the rest no matter who owns the enterprise.

The alienation that is religious belief and hope will also disappear along with the real alienation of economic life, since economic events determine all others (p.89). But Marx appears to be concerned that the idea of Creation may still occur to men, who find it hard to conceive of man and nature existing through themselves, for their own lives are ones of dependence upon other people and things. The regression to a First Cause, which Marx takes only in a temporal sense, seems inevitable. Marx answers that the question, Who created the first man and the world as a whole?, is 'inverted' in supposing that man and nature do not exist and in asking for a proof that they do exist. It abstracts from man and the world, and this abstraction should be given up or made consistent so that the questioner, along with man and the world, is thought of as non-existent. 'Do not think, do not ask me questions, for immediately you think and ask, your abstraction from the being of man and nature has no meaning' (pp.94–5). It seems then, from this transparently fallacious argument, that man and nature just have to be accepted as being there and that we must not raise any questions about this fact. 'Socialist man' in any case has no need for such questioning and thinking, since he takes world history to be 'nothing but the creation of man by human labour and the development of nature for man'. (There are echoes here of Hegel's teleology, of his notion of the world as existing as the not–self necessary for Spirit in and through man to become conscious of itself.) And this will become evident in his practical life, when alienation has been overcome through the collective appropriation and control of the means of human life, and so the idea of an alien being above nature and man will become practically impossible (p.95).

Elsewhere (p.104) Marx offers a metaphysical argument for his 'naturalism or humanism'. Briefly, this is that only objective beings, ones with objects outside themselves on which they depend, can exist. If a non-objective being existed, it would exist alone, for otherwise it would be the object of another being and have that other being as its object. 'As soon as I have an object, this object then has me as an object', and so a non-objective can be only imagined and not an object of sense–perception and so real. (This argument assumes that being an object is a reciprocal relationship, like being a brother or sister, and that being an object implies some sort of dependence or being affected, assumptions we may well wish to question.) It therefore rules out a transcendent Creator, but whether it rules out Hegel's immanent Spirit is another matter, for, like Spinoza's *Deus sive Natura* and the Absolutes of Bradley and Bosanquet, the latter includes its objects within itself. Perhaps Marx envisages nature–with–man as an all–inclusive and self–originating system, and thus as the one, non–objective being. Certainly some of his terminology suggests such a possibility.

So much for Marx's general conception of man and the world. What then follows regarding education? I suggest that to answer that question we must distinguish three stages to which a Marxist theory is applied: (a) education as it has been, now is and will be for the immediate future in the state of human alienation; (b) education as it will be in the state immediately after the Revolution when private property has been merely abolished; and (c) education as it will finally be when alienation has been totally overcome. In addition, there is the problem for Marxist theorists of reconciling theory with fact as the facts fail to conform to Marx's prognosis.

Now Marx himself wrote very little about education, and so it has been left to his successors to apply his general theories to education, and in so doing they have mostly been concerned with (a) except when they have held that in the former USSR or China or somewhere else events have moved on to stage (b), and little appears to have been written by anyone about (c) [8]. Since we are concerned with Marx's general account of man and the world, and not with the details of his accounts of society, economics and history, we are interested in what that general account implies as regards the general nature and orientation of education, and thus with (c) more than a Marxist account of and prescription for education in stages (a) and (b). Yet there is one important thing to be said about education in the pre–Revolutionary era: that, curiously like Christianity, formal education is irrelevant to the salvation of man in the Marxist drama. To maintain that teaching people about their lot, spreading ideas about it, will by itself lead to radical change, would be to relapse into the Idealist illusion that ideas can change reality, and to abandon the Revolution for Revisionism, cataclysmic change for gradual amelioration. It is men's material and economic conditions which determine ideas and beliefs, and not vice–versa. And so the Revolution, which in Marx's and other modern mythologies is the mystical means of transforming man and the world, will come about, not through the extension of schooling and enlightenment, but through the progressive pauperisation of the workers in visible contrast to their productive capacity and the accumulation of wealth and culture for property-owners [9]. Thus it is the class-struggle and not the class-room which is the motive power of radical change. Yet Communists can, as the vanguard of the proletariat, enlighten the latter as to their real condition and the course of the future (impart the Marxist gnosis) and mobilize them for the Revolution [1Ø], work to which Marx himself turned (in contrast to the Quietist acceptance of events which Hegelianism seems to imply). The Revolution can be aided but cannot be created by such means. Consequently, Marxism is not one of those movements in modern times which expects the extension of formal education to be a principal vehicle for change, since education itself is part of the superstructure that is conditioned by, and does not act upon, the material and economic base of society. Nor did Marx envisage the control and manipulation of the rest of the population as practised by Marxist and other régimes, in which those in control are tacitly exempted from the domination by circumstances ('environment') ascribed explicitly to all: 'circumstances are changed by men and it is necessary to educate the educator himself' [11], that is, to change his circumstances. The question immediately arises, as we shall see that it does also for B.F.Skinner, of *who* can do this.

One other comment on education before the Revolution: there is an ambiguity in what Marxism would prescribe for such conditions. On the one hand, it could prescribe improvements in the education of the proletariat, in keeping with its ultimate aims, and in order to enlighten the proletarians about their real condition, its causes and cure [12]. But, on the other hand, it could equally require working-class education, like the rest of working-class life, to become and be made progressively worse, so as to hasten the day when the proletariat is finally driven to universal revolt. (Radicals and revolutionaries usually have an ambiguous attitude towards the alleviation or aggravation of present ills, for, like wise Conservatives, they know that the existing order can be maintained by giving rising sections of the population more of a stake in it.) Perhaps both could be done by Marxist propaganda and agitation within the system, which could combat any elements of 'false consciousness' among the children of the workers, while undermining and disrupting the system generally.

Yet what about the achievement of Socialist society and Socialist man, when alienation is finally overcome, there is no strict division of labour, the realm of necessity is greatly reduced and men produce mainly from a free desire so to do? What then would be the aims and tasks of education?

From Marx's own comments, noted above, about the worker now feeling free only in his merely animal activities, we can safely infer that Marx would not see the purpose of education as preparing the young just for a life of amusement, indulgence and fun. Marx saw man as a producer but he has not been the only one to see work as man's essential activity, in contrast to Aristotle's focus upon contemplation: for example, Eric Gill, whose ideal was the craftsman and therefore, unlike Marx, wanted more to retreat from modern industry than to continue it in new circumstances [13]. But whereas Gill saw the aim of work to be the greater glory of God, for Marx work could only be the self-expression and self-development of man, individually and collectively, with no other aim or purpose. On the one hand, Marx emphasizes the social nature of all activity, even when not intentionally nor obviously social, as we noted above; yet, on the other hand, he saw Socialist society as the liberation of individuality by means of the abolition of the division of labour [14]. Presumably Marx would not see any tension here, and would hold the development of man to be simultaneously individual and collective. In any case, it has no aim beyond itself, for Reality consists only of man and Nature, man using and expressing himself through his activity within and upon Nature, and Nature being humanised by man.

Since man, in Marx's view, is essentially a producer, education would then be designed to increase the capacities of the young for spontaneous production, nor, we may presume, would there be much need for compulsion, since work would no longer be alienated from the worker and since men are workers (if Marx is correct). Socialist society would liberate the urge to work and so would have no problems of incentives or compulsion. One error we must avoid here: Marx was not Dewey, and did not, in principle at any rate, confine work and production to economic, industrial and commercial activities, though he wrote most about these. In so far as they comprise the realm of necessity, never to be eliminated in human life, then there would always be a need for a specifically economic, industrial, agricultural and commercial education. And Marx did call for a combination of education with industrial production and approved of the provisions, in this respect, of the English Factory Acts [15]. But production for Marx applied to all human activities the production of art and science no less than of shoes and machinery. We would therefore expect unalienated education, not so much to teach the young to produce things, but to teach them how to produce what they freely wish to produce. And we would expect it to teach them how to *produce* rather than how to consume or contemplate.

The combination of education and work, as Marx saw it already happening, pointed the way out of 'detail work' whereby the worker is confined to one, highly specific operation. A wider education would permit the worker to do more than one thing and so the more to fulfil himself in his work. But in that passage already quoted, wherein he envisaged the final overcoming of the specialisation of labour, he put it only in the rural, agricultural and pastoral terms in which it first arose. Yet Marx wished both to overcome the division of labour and to maintain modern industry. In his day a Brunel might perhaps design a steam locomotive, build a ship and bridge a river, and then criticize after dinner. But today, and increasingly so, many occupations are more intellectually demanding and so require extensive and *specialist* training such that few can successfully take up more than one, even successively let alone simultaneously. And Marx would not regard as appropriate to man's essence the many low- and no-tech jobs that exist in catering and other services. Which way, then, should the economy and education go: for all-round development, competence in many spheres and a simpler, craft and non-industrial economy, à *la* William Morris; or for industrialism, technical expertise and specialist training?

Moreover, we may question the feasability of everyone together planning everything and that with the freedom to take up, and change occupations as one wishes. Even more so we may question the compatibility of this democratic collectivism with Marx's forecast of the withering away of the institutions of government. And apart from such pragmatic difficulties in overcoming 'alienation', there is a deeper problem. For, it seems, what Marx ultimately meant by 'alienation' was finite, determinate and particular existence, being *this* and not *that*, being *this sort* of thing or person and not *that sort*. Recall his opposition to the division of labour and all roles. Consider also his selection of the German proletariat, and not the civil service which was Hegel's choice, as the 'universal class' free from special interests, and the way he described it [16]. It is universal in having no definite character and therefore no definite interests. It claims 'no *particular* right' for it suffers no '*particular wrong* but wrong in *general*', and it has no '*historical* title' but only a '*human* one'. This is the same fallacy of the abstract universal which we met in Rousseau who wanted Emile to be merely a man and not any sort of man. Consequently no actual state of affairs, no class, no individual and no work can ever become unalienated. The result, as Hegel saw with reference to Rousseau and the French Revolution, can only be destructive, as everything that exists and comes into existence is resented as alien, unwilled by oneself, differentiated, determinate and particular. What Marx really wanted to do was to liberate men from the conditions of all finite existence [17]. That was also implicit in the Gnosticism of old. For, when the sparks of Light or fragments of Spirit have divested themselves of the encrustations which separate them from the One Light or Spirit, and have escaped from the world, there is then nothing to distinguish them from each other nor from that One Light or Spirit. Hence, in the End as in the Beginning, there will only be the Light or the Spirit. But for Marx there is no other world and life, and so there is no escape from alienation. As we shall see, Sartre drew that conclusion.

Marx tried to provide a new understanding of man, emphasising his role as a worker and his collective existence, to fill the void left by the absence of any transcendent Law or Way. We now turn to Nietzsche's radically Individualist vision of the creative few.

Notes

1. *Karl Marx: Selected Writings*, ed. McLellan, pp.164-5.
2. *Capital*, end of Preface to the second edition.
3. ibid. pp.12-3. Marx omits Hermes' reply, 'This is madness'.
4. ibid. pp.63-4.
5. *Karl Marx: Selected Writings in Sociology and Social Philosophy*, ed. Bottomore and Rubel, p.78.
6. McLellan, pp.77-87, 87-96, respectively. The following references in the text are to this volume.
7. Bottomore and Rubel, pp.259-6∅.
8. See B. Simon, 'Problems in Contemporary Educational Theory: A Marxist Approach', *JPE*, Vol.12, 1978.
9. McLellan, pp.134-5, 227.
1∅. ibid. p.231; cf. pp.574-5.
11. ibid. p.156
12. But see, ibid. p.538 on the present improvement of the worker and his education by means of trades unions.
13. See Eric Gill, *A Holy Tradition of Working.*
14. McLellan, pp.19∅-1. Note (ibid. p.19∅ and the end of the section preceding it) that there would be 'no painters, but at most people who engage in painting among other activities'. Marx, while defining men as workers, would not have anyone define himself in terms of any one type of work. We found the same refusal of roles in Rousseau; we shall find it again in Sartre; and in a weaker form (of choosing all roles for oneself) it is implied in the theory of Rational Autonomy, which we shall consider in Chap. 7. But may not some people want to be painters, only painters and nothing else?
15. ibid. p.237; Bottomore and Rubel, p.259.
16. *Critique of Hegel's Philosophy of Right*, in *Early Writings*, trans. Livingstone and Berton, p.256.
17. See also the Marxist 'Critical Theory' of Adorno, Horkheimer and others, and its application to education, which results in a desire to 'emancipate' the young from any definite roles, way of life and beliefs, as summarised by R. Young in *A Critical Theory of Education*, Chap. 3.

6 Nietzsche: The breeding of higher men and creators of values

Marx presents a collective view of man, mankind as defining itself through work and the process of history. In contrast Nietzsche gives us an Individualist view of a cultural élite defining both themselves and others. Of course, that is what Marxism comes to in practice, the Party and its leaders determining what everyone else is to do and to be. But Nietzsche explicitly distinguishes between the creative minority of cultural innovators who invent 'the tablets of stone' which the majority, 'the herd', takes for its law. This interpretation of man is developed in Nietzsche's later works, those from *The Gay Science* onwards. Thus we shall omit his earlier writings on education, which have been studied elsewhere, and restrict ourselves to the later works which develop and apply his wider views of man and the world [1].

Nietzsche leaves us in no doubt that he rejects the older form of cosmology, in the specific shape of Christian Theism. Zarathrustra descends to announce that 'God is dead' (*Z* Prologue 2; cf *GS* 125). Man is therefore left without supernatural guidance. What is he to do? To acquire the strength needed to live without God (*GS* 285) and also without a morality that is given to us, a Law that we have not made. Morality has been 'unmasked' and is shown to be without any basis. Therefore we are 'to invent new tablets of what is good' and '*to become what we are* – human beings who are unique, incomparable, who give themselves laws, who create themselves' (*GS* 335). But this is a task possible only for the few. It means being like a camel, able to bear burdens; then like a lion, to conquer freedom, to fight the dragon of 'Thou shalt' (imposed and extraneous laws), and to create the freedom needed for creation; and then like a child, to create values themselves *Z*, I:1). Man is thus to be a bridge between the animal realm and the overman, the creator of values, who is yet to come (*Z* Prologue, 3,4). Today men cannot create the overman, but they can make themselves the fathers and forefathers of the overman (*Z* II: 2), that is, into 'higher men'. That, in essence, is Nietzsche's message. Let us now look at some of its details.

Nietzsche appears to be an anti-metaphysician but what he criticizes is a form of metaphysics, that which divides Reality into two worlds, applies moral evaluations to them, and so blames the one (especially this world) for not being the other and yearns for a 'Beyond' (*WP* 17, 18, 574, 579, 583-6; cf *Z* I:3, II:19,2∅; *BGE* 2). To this *ressentiment* against existence, earthly existence, Nietzsche opposes 'the innocence of becoming' (*TI* p.5∅1), a re-affirmation of Heraclitus' teaching that all is flux (*Z* III: 12 (8)), and 'the eternal recurrence of the same' (*GS* 341; *Z* III: 2; *WP* 617, 1∅58-67). Like the child, we should 'yes' to whatever is (*Z* I:3; cf *TI* p.561). Another name for this is *amor fati*, 'love of fate', love of whatever one is and whatever one encounters, 'a Dionysian relationship to existence' (*WP* 1∅41; *GS* IV; *EH* II: 1∅, III). This includes acceptance of the recurrence throughout infinite time of every event exactly as it has already happened. This later idea came to Nietzsche as a great revelation, yet its precise significance is hard to decipher, and it seems to be valued as a test of one's psychological strength, of one's ability to hold it to be true and to rejoice and not despair in it (*WP* 1∅6∅). He tried to argue for it (*WP* 1∅62, 1∅64, 1∅66), but his argument depended upon the category of cause which, along that of free will (one's own causeless causality), he rejected as devices for blaming the world (*TI* 'The Four Great Idols'; *BGE* 21). Hume also had rejected the notion of cause (which, as we saw, Kant tried to re-instate), and again like Hume [2], Nietzsche also rejected the idea of a substantive and permanent soul and interpreted the soul as a society of instincts struggling for mastery (*BGE* 12, 19, 54; *WP* 49∅, 492).

Nietzsche thus opposes the modern forms of Gnosticism which condemn the present and look for a radically different future in this world, and there is no sense of alienation in his work. Yet he too, for all his invocation of 'eternal recurrence' and 'innocence of becoming', nevertheless looks to the future, to the birth of the Overman, and would have the present orientated to that goal.

His own positive interpretation of Reality is that it, and man, are 'will to power'. This idea he found in Helvetius, 'the last great event in morals' (*WP* 248), at whom we shall look in Chapter 8. Helvetius took the will to power to be the basic drive in man which underlies all other desires and emotions. Nietzsche held that the will to power is especially shown in overcoming or surpassing oneself. Moreover he applied to nature and man, to individuals, forces within them, society, moral systems, art, knowledge and philosophy as its most spiritual form (*WP* Bk III; *BGE* 9, 32). His vision of the world is of it as fixed in size, a play of forces, eternally creating and transforming itself, a '*Dionysian* world', '"beyond good and evil", without goal, unless the joy of the circle is itself a goal, without will'. '*This world is the will to power – and nothing besides!* And you yourselves are also this will to power – and nothing besides!' (*WP* 1∅67).

But, as may already be apparent, Nietzsche is not concerned with any detached consideration of what the world and man are but with the valuations which, he thinks, lie behind all world-views. In particular, he fears the reaction of one sort of 'Nihilism' to the new, godless conception of the world. What he seeks to do is not to revert to any traditional cosmology, but to go beyond Nihilism as it now is to a more radical and joyful form. He repudiates the Nihilism that is *disappointed* that God no longer exists, that morality has undone itself (honesty, a part of morality, now requires that we see that morality has no foundation – *GM* III 27), that values have no reality, and that the world has no meaning (*WP* 1). Thus Nihilism means that '*the highest values devaluate themselves.* The aim is lacking; "Why?" finds no answer' (*WP* 2). He does not repudiate any of these propositions, only the despair and destructiveness to which they usually lead. Despairing Nihilism arises from three sets of beliefs: (a) that the world-process aims at something, and then that it aims at and achieves nothing; (b) a belief in totality, unity and dependence upon a superior whole, and then the realisation that there is no such whole; and (c) from the former two, an escape from this world to an invented 'true' world beyond it, which is then seen through, and yet one still cannot endure this world to which 'aim', 'unity' and 'being' cannot be applied, and which appears valueless (*WP* 12). (We shall find an example of this response in Sartre's Existentialism.) In accordance with his interpretation of the world as will to power, as life and thus as increasing or decreasing strength, Nietzsche regards Nihilism as ambiguous: it can be the despairing, pessimist and passive form as just described, and thus a sign of decreased power; or take an active and accepting form and be a sign of increased power (*WP* 22). It is the latter which Nietzsche advocates, the active taking up and willing of the world as meaningless in itself.

This involves two contradictory and equally illogical valuations by Nietzsche: that *power* is the basis of all value (*WP* 54, 382, 713), and the injunction to create values. These are contradictory, since, if power or strength is the basis of all value, then the only values that can be created are new species of power, and Nietzsche never himself created any new values but fell back upon older ones, as we shall see. And these are both illogical on Nietzsche's premises, which are that morality has overcome itself, that values are unfounded, and thus that there are 'no moral phenomena, there is only a moral interpretation of these phenomena' (*WP* 258; *BGE* 108; *TI* p.501). Like others since, Nietzsche deduces from the mere factuality of the world a moral valuation or injunction – rather two: that, since Reality is will to power, power is value and *should* be valued; and that, since there are no values, we *should* create new ones or help to breed those who will create them. In Chapter 7 we shall meet a contemporary form of the same fallacy – and from professed 'Anti-Naturalists'! – viz. that, since there are no values in things and since our value-judgments are merely subjective opinions, we *should* not impose them upon the young. But, if values are unfounded, then so are Nietzsche's and so is his call to create them. And it is clear that Nietzsche is putting these forward as *moral* evaluations and injunctions, and not just as personal suggestions or preferences.

Nietzsche's attacks upon morality are attacks upon a specific form of it, what he calls 'slave morality', in favour of another form, 'master morality'. Since moral systems are forms or expressions of the will to power, they are to be understood via 'genealogy', by way of the way in which they have arisen, the motives and intentions behind them. Despite his acknowledgment that an enquiry into origins is not a refutation (*WP* 254), Nietzsche is in fact engaged in a Reductionist debunking. Morality – the morality of benevolence and sympathy – is discredited by showing (he claims) that it stems from *ressentiment*, the desire of the weak to prove themselves superior to, to revenge themselves upon, and to bind the strong (*GM* passim; *WP* 401; *BGE* 260). Also, Nietzsche claims, all attempts to improve and moralise mankind involve means which are immoral, i.e. by the standards of the morality of benevolence (*TI* 'The "Improvers of Mankind"'; *WP* 317). That morality is a movement against 'the efforts of nature to achieve a higher type' (*WP* 306, 311, 400). Therefore what Nietzsche means by 'beyond good and evil' is the rejection of what is ordinarily understood as morally good and evil in favour of 'good and bad', 'noble and base', and 'noble and despicable' in terms of life and thus strength and power, and especially of superfluity of strength, the morality of masters and rulers (*BGE* 260).

Nietzsche upholds 'master morality', that of the strong, Nature itself, the will to power accepted as such. He values the 'moraline-free' *virtù* of the Renaissance, not the *virtue* of the pure in heart (*WP* 317; *A* 2). It is valuation of power and strength, especially psychological strength. He evaluates a man by the power of his will, and that in turn by 'the resistance, pain, torture it endures and knows how to turn to its advantage'. ' I do not account the evil and painful character of existence a reproach to it, but hope rather that it will one day be more evil and painful than hitherto' (*WP* 382; cf 1041 on worth as how much one can endure and dare). Again, he teaches 'the No to all that makes weak – that exhausts' and 'the Yes to all that strengthens, that stores up strength, that justifies the feeling of strength' (*WP* 54; cf *A* 2). The value of the individual is thus that of the accumulation in him of an ascending line of life; but, should he manifest 'decay, chronic degeneration, and sickness', then he is of little worth, should take as little as possible from 'those who have turned out well' and upon whom he is a parasite (*TI* p.534; *WP* 373). Hence Nietzsche is indifferent to what would ordinarily be called the evil actions, or evil effects of the actions, of 'higher men' such as Caesar and Napoleon (*WP* 1017; cf 1025 on culture requiring the use of 'everything terrible'). Great good requires, uses and produces great evil (*Z* II: 12). He justifies by reference to the practice of Nature, lack of pity for the degenerate: rights to altruism, help and equality of condition have no basis in physiology, and are 'prizes for the degenerate and underprivileged' (*WP* 52).

Strength is to be understood primarily as psychological strength. This can be expressed in two somewhat opposed ways: by a pruning of the self to let one instinct predominate and so to be strong in a specific way; and by expanding the self to take in more and antithetical drives and ideas yet without disintegrating, of which Goethe was an outstanding example (*BGE* 200, 213, 260; *TI* pp. 545-6, 553-4; *WP* 966-7).

Power is also shown in mastery, and thus what in the Renaissance was called *sprezzatura*, a word, which, for all his admiration of Italy and the Renaissance, I have not found in Nietzsche. Yet it expresses what he referred to as 'dancing', that complete mastery of an art which hides all art and seems totally effortless (*Z* III:2, 15, 16; cf *WP* 430 on education in morality as always aiming at producing 'the certainty of instinct').

Another aspect of Nietzsche's 'more severe morality' is that it rests solely on the will of the individual, is a direct expression of his desire, and has no pretentions to 'justification'. It is the self-certainty of the 'noble soul' in its own rightness simply because it does what it does (*GE* 260, 265; *A* 11).

As can already be seen, Nietzsche totally rejects all notions of equality (*Z* II: 7). He denies that mankind is a whole, and by implication that it has a single task or goal (*WP* 339) and the idea of a common good (*BGE* 43, 62). 'Common' in his vocabulary means 'shared' (and thus 'public' in the Wittgensteinian vocabulary of our contemporary philosophy of education) and therefore 'commonplace' and 'vulgar' (*BGE* 268). In contrast, he upholds an 'ordering of rank' and therefore not 'an individualistic morality', i.e. one in which every individual counts equally(*WP* 287; cf 784 against Individualism and the Socialism which it uses, and 752 against democratic egalitarianism). It is quanta of strength and power, being on ascending and not declining lines of life, which determine one's value and order of rank. This means that the person simply as a person counts for nothing: the individual is 'something quite new who creates new things' (*WP* 767) and the 'personality' is a rare occurrence (*WP* 886)--neither belongs to any and every person, only the outstanding few. It also means that some count for much more than others according to their quanta of power and their representing higher stages of life. Now Nietzsche applies this in two ways: to individuals and to classes. Ultimately, his ideal is the overman who creates values; mediately it is the 'higher men' who create the conditions wherein the overman may emerge; and proximately it is aristocracies in the social sense, ruling classes, especially those who rule with a clear conscience, with confidence in themselves, and do not seek spurious justifications such as pity, benevolence and the good of others whereby they pretend to be obeying (a law) rather than commanding (*BGE* 199). Hence Nietzsche praises 'healthy' (self-confident) aristocracies, and aristocratic attitudes and virtues (*BGE* IX; *WP* 942-951). It could appear that, on his own principles, he should value only outstanding individuals and not any class, the psychological strength shown by certain persons and not the political power exercised by any group. But he holds that the latter is the breeding ground for the former. And, since the above constitutes Nietzsche's ideal for life and education, we can now turn to the breeding of higher men as its means.

Such men are to be commanders and law-givers, primarily through creating values and setting new tablets of virtues, rather than through political control. Indeed, those who create the values are, in effect, the powers behind the thrones and the users of the rulers (*WP* 998). What, then, is needed to be a commander and creator of values? Psychological strength, as we have seen, joyfully to face the meaninglessness of life, the void of values that one is to fill, and thus to be sceptical (*WP* 963; *A* 54 - contrast the scepticism that is a sign of weakness and debility *BGE* 208); therefore the ability to be solitary, incommunicable and uncommon (*BGE* 284; *WP* 886, 985); aristocratic consciousness of one's superiority - looking across to a few acknowledged equals and down upon the rest, and, let us note, never up, for there is nothing higher than himself (*BGE* 265, 286-7); the willingness to rule, to use the 'herd', to accept great evil for great good, like Caesar and Napoleon; the ability to include many drives in great strength without being torn apart by them.

We may list the means for producing these qualities under the two headings of social arrangements and discipline.

Firstly, the requisite social arrangements, primarily a distinction, and increasingly sharper distinction, between the 'higher men' or 'noble souls', or the ranks from whom they emerge, and the 'herd' or everyone else. The herd is all those who lack the potentiality for being creators or ancestors of creators. The herd lives according to the moral laws, the tables of virtue, laid down by the creative minority. 'The ideas of the herd should rule in the herd - but not reach out beyond it' (*WP* 287). Let us note here what us required for the education of the herd and the 'virtues' which are to be implanted in them: 'Absolute commands; terrible means of compulsion; to tear them away from the easy life'; they are to obey but, because of their vanity, may have to think that they obey 'principles' rather than the commands of great men (*WP* 764). Yet Nietzsche can also say that it needs to learn reverence for authority, and gives the example of the Bible in Europe in instilling discipline and refining manners, though the continued influence of such books depends upon 'an external tyranny of authority'. But, we may ask, would not such a mode of authority be sheer power instead and so not generate reverence? Any way, the masses need to learn that there are things they must not touch, while the modern intellectual needs to acquire a sense of shame (*BGE* 263). The herd is disciplined by conforming to laws which it does not originate. Such a mass at the bottom of society is required, Nietzsche thinks, to give the culture-producing minority that necessary sense of distance and superiority. A high culture can stand only on a broad base, 'upon a strong and healthy consolidated mediocrity' (*WP* 864). The mediocre fail to understand the necessity for evil, and desire ideals without any harmful, dangerous and destructive aspects; but the growth of good involves the growth of evil; and most people are fragmentary, not synthetic, and so are merely preludes and rehearsals for the exceptional man who can unite diverse elements (*WP* 881). The members of the herd are gregarious and common but higher men are solitary and unique. They need a sense of difference, and the growing homogenization of man in industrial Europe in fact will aid the emergence of higher men by widening the actual gulf and so increasing that sense of difference (*WP* 886; cf 8901-2). The clockwork of the new economy dwarfs men and makes them adaptable, and, to compensate, a reverse movement is necessary - the production of 'a synthesizing, summarising, justifying man for whose existence the transformation of mankind into a machine is a precondition, as a base on which he can invent *his higher form of living*' (*WP* 866; cf 890, 898, 901). The lower exist for the sake of the higher, and not vice-versa as humanitarianism holds (*WP* 901). Nietzsche teaches that there are higher and lower men, and that 'a single individual can justify the existence of whole millenia - that is, a full, rich, great, whole human being in relation to countless incomplete fragmentary men' (*WP* 997). It is a fundamental error 'to place the goal in the herd and not in single individuals', for 'the herd is a means, no more!' (*WP* 766). 'Not "mankind" but the *overman* is the goal!' (*WP* 1001).

Also, it seems, a higher class is necessary, for, Nietzsche holds, higher men take generations to be bred. He uses 'breeding' in both the biological sense and in that of 'good up-bringing'. It is the 'storing up of the tremendous forces of mankind so that the generations can build upon the work of their forefathers' in producing the stronger and breeding out the weak (*WP* 398). The nobility of noble souls derives only from a nobility of birth and blood, not of spirit, for something must ennoble spirit (*WP* 942). Heredity is superior to education, and in this democratic age education is deceiving plebians in body and soul about their origins (*WP* 264).

Within the higher class, we can distinguish two levels of the training of individuals: that which produces or reproduces higher men, and that which goes further to produce the creators of values.

In respect of the former, Nietzsche recommends a 'a rigorous polytechnic education', with military service, so that the men in the higher classes would be officers (*WP* 793). The point of this, presumably, is that thereby they would learn obeying and commanding. 'Freedom, subtlety, boldness, dance and masterly certainty', in thought and action, stem from prolonged obedience to arbitary laws, an otherwise pointless discipline (*BGE* 188). Hard discipline, at the right time, is needed: when 'it still makes one proud to see that much is demanded of one'. A good school, for which there is no substitute, is a hard one: it 'demands much and sternly so; demands even good and exceptional as norm; praise rare, indulgence non-existent; blame apportioned sharply, objectively, without regard for talents or antecedents'. Soldiers and scholars are produced by this same discipline, and have the same qualities: ability to command, and pride in obeying, preferring danger to comfort, not to weigh what is allowed and what is forbidden 'on a shop-keeper's scales', 'to be a foe more of the petty, sly, parasitic, than of the evil. – What does one learn in a hard school? Obeying and commanding' (*WP* 912). What Nietzsche wants is the training that would produce a cultural SAS. But a military training also instills *ésprit de corps*, and that, as Miss Jean Brodie said of 'team spirit', is for the rest of the cast and not the star, the lower and not the really higher men. The discipline of the latter would have to go beyond it.

Those who are to create values and to fashion men according to 'the pleasure of a creative and profound will' will employ 'law-giving moralities' and work upon the masses like artists, so that for centuries their will will prevail in the shape of 'laws, religions and customs'. But it will also take many life-times to produce such men. Hence the need for a new aristocracy 'based on severest self-legislation, in which the will of philosophical men of power and artist-tyrants will be able to endure for millenia' (*WP* 96∅). It will in fact require 'iron men who have never yet lived' to create the conditions necessary for the eventual emergence of the overman (*WP* 9∅8). The solution, it seems, presupposes that the problem has already been solved. But in several passages Nietzsche indicates something of what is needed, and that is more a self-training or shaping by events, rather than a formal education. Many, we may expect, will be tested and found wanting. They will be tested by suffering to see how much they can endure (*WP* 91∅; *BGE* 225, 27∅), and as noted previously, by isolation and solitariness, how much they can encompass without disintegration, by their strength in relying on themselves alone and facing the meaninglessness of life without despair, for they are to give life its meaning by creating values upon which others can more comfortably rely.

This task Nietzsche assigns to philosophers, not the Kantian nor (we may add) the Analytic philosopher, but 'the Caesarian cultivator and *Gewaltmensch* of culture', a strong man dominating by violence (*BGE* 2∅7). Such philosophers go beyond scholarship, the ascertaining of valuations which men have made, to legislating such valuations and without claiming that their '"This shall be!" is God's or reflects "eternal values"' (*WP* 972). They will have to reverse accepted valuations and to teach men that they must rely on human will alone and prepare them for 'great enterprises and collective experiments in discipline and breeding' in order to end the 'gruesome dominion of chance and nonsense that has hitherto been called "history"' (*BGE* 2Ø3). The requirements for such philosophers are specified further in Part Six, 'We Scholars' of the same work, to which I shall refer the reader.

In the last quoted, and very explicit statement, Nietzsche ends up in the same position as virtually all the new Gnostic interpreters of the world: viz. itching to control it and remould it anew. Hegel himself, confident that reason rules the world, felt no temptation to take over as reason incarnate, but Marx and his followers did feel, and succumb to, the temptation to move history further and faster along its predestined course. And, in his frank recognition that they will impose upon the masses their will simply as their will in the forms of values and laws which they create *ex nihilo* and by sheer fiat, Nietzsche honestly admits, in effect, that his creators of values will be Conditioners, whereas Professor Skinner, as we shall see in Chapter 8, tries to escape from that charge.

We can now see that, as suggested above, Nietzsche himself was not an overman who created new values. Rather, he reverted to old ones, those of Homer's heroes. Could this be, as C.S. Lewis said [3], because men can invent new values no more than they can imagine new primary colours? R. Solomon has suggested another difficulty: that there was no existing practice to which Nietzsche could point as exemplifying his valuations [4]. If correct, that would be an inhibition on overmen, or, rather, on their emergence in the first place, for the relevant practice would have to arise first. And Professor MacIntyre has suggested that no practice is possible for Nietzsche's doctrine of *self*-assertion, and that the Homeric heroes to whom he turns instead fulfilled and asserted their *roles* (defined beforehand) [5].

But if men, even overmen, cannot create values, then perhaps they can choose them from the stock of existing beliefs. Let us now turn to a theory of education based on that proposal.

Notes

1. References to Nietzsche's works will be given in the text using the following abbreviations, with paragraph numbers except where as stated here:
    A   = *The Antichrist*
    BGE = *Beyond Good and Evil*
    EH   = *Ecce Homo*
    GS   = *The Gay Science*
    GM   = *The Genealogy of Morals*
    TI   = *The Twilight of the Idols*, plus page numbers
    WP   = *The Will to Power*
    Z   = *Thus Spake Zarathustra*, plus Part and section numbers.
    Quotations from all these, except for *BGE* and *WP*, are taken from *The Portable Nietzsche*.
2. See N. Davey, 'Nietzsche and Hume on Self and Identity', *Journal of the British Society for Phenomenology*, Vol. 18, No. 1, Jan. 1987.
3. *The Abolition of Man*, p.3Ø.
4. 'A More Severe Morality: Nietzsche's Affirmative Ethics', *Journal of the British Society for Phenomenology*, Vol. 16, No. 3, Oct. 1985.
5. *After Virtue*, p.122.

7 Contemporary theory and Sartre: Rational autonomy and nothingness condemned to choose

We turn now firstly, not to one philosopher, but to a group, and not to a version of man as self-defining subject in a meaningless universe which is then expressed in a view of education, but with a view of education from which we shall draw out the cosmology and anthropology assumed by it. That is, we turn to the thesis that one of the main aims of education, or specifically of moral education, is to promote rational autonomy. This has been presented, by name or otherwise, in many books and articles [1]. It articulates the dominant assumptions of contemporary theory of education. In Britain it lay behind the Schools' Council's Humanities Project and its prescription of the neutral chairmanship by the teacher of discussions of moral and social issues wherein he would teach only the methods of rational discussion [2]. It also lay behind the change from RE, the authoritative teaching of Christianity, to RS, the uncommitted teaching of 'World Religions' or 'Stances for Living', as a menu from which the pupils may select and reject as they please. In North America it is present in the theory and widespread practice of Values Clarification, according to which the pupils are not be taught ('indoctrinated' with) any set of values but are to be encouraged to 'clarify' their own existing sets of values whatever they may be [3], and in the developmental theory of Lawrence Kohlberg in which the final stage is a semi-Kantian self-chosen set of abstract, consistent and universal principles of justice, and the aim of education is to promote progression to the next higher stage [4]. And R. Young, in his *A Critical Theory of Education: Habermas and our Children's Future*, has derived substantially similar conclusions from the Critical Theory of the Frankfurt School (Adorno, Horkheimer) and the philosophy of Jürgen Habermas.

Behind all these theories and practices we note the common and fundamental assumption that there is no concrete set of moral laws, political arrangements and religious beliefs which can be known to be true and so could be legitimately taught. And we also note the commom consequences drawn from that assumption: that the young are not to be left as they are, as Radical critics of these theories and proposals desire, but are to be helped to make their own choices in a *rational* manner; and so that the young are to be taught *formal* principles, and any necessary information, by which they can make rational choices. We shall focus on the theorists of Rational Autonomy for, by and large, they have spelt out more clearly the assumptions and principles behind their rejection of traditional 'indoctrination' and their alternative schemes.

Yet they have gone only so far, because of their self–denying ordinance with regard to metaphysics. Therefore we shall then review Sartre's Existentialist account of man, wherein, in effect, the view of man and the world implied in the theory of Rational Autonomy is fully articulated and its consequences are elaborated, with a few but very significant sentences on education.

Many, perhaps most, of those who hold and present the theory of Rational Autonomy would deny that it followed from or implied any metaphysical account of the world and of man's place in it. Indeed, it is part of their view of education that such matters are not to be authoritatively taught but are, instead, to be topics upon which the young are to be taught rationally to make up their own minds. And, in contemporary philosophy of education, metaphysics is mentioned but rarely and then only to be dismissed or ignored. Positivism, it seems, still continues to exert a powerful influence. But, as I have argued elsewhere [5], we cannot escape metaphysical commitments neither in the theory nor the practice of education. And the thesis that the young are to be taught to make up their own minds about religious or other world–views, and moral and political beliefs and practices, manifestly presumes that the world itself sets us and them no Law or Way for the individual and society to follow, so that we and they must define our own. It assumes also that Reality is confined to the universe and that it is also essentially neutral. This is expressed in the dogmas that values cannot be deduced from facts nor ethics from metaphysics, which it has taken over from Analytic moral philosophy. What, then, if anything, may or should we teach? The theory of Rational Autonomy is the articulation of that problem and the attempt, without questioning the never stated metaphysical framework in which it arises, to find some way out for a rational and morally respectable education.

It is important to distinguish, as perhaps some theorists do not, this doctrine of Rational Autonomy from other ideas of personal autonomy. As traditionally understood, personal autonomy is a matter of emotional maturity, self–reliance and moral integrity: respectively, not being so emotionally dependent on another that one cannot decide anything for oneself; the ability and the will to organise oneself and one's life and not to rely on others to provide for oneself; and the ability and will to be resolute and to stand by one's convictions. Such traits of character are promoted by an education that sets them forth as authoritative virtues, present in historical or fictional models, inspired by living examples, and inculcated through the ethos and atmosphere of home and school: i.e. by a thorough–going 'indoctrination'. The theorists of Rational Autonomy go beyond such an ideal to something radically different: to the notion that the young are to determine their own moral, political, religious or non–religious, and perhaps other beliefs, principles and practices, for there are none that can be authoritatively presented to them.

I shall now summarise the common elements in those works wherein, explicitly or implicitly Rational Autonomy, is presented as an ideal for education, and I shall note in passing particular variations or additions:
1. The teaching of any substantive moral, political or religious (or metaphysical) beliefs is 'indoctrination', for all such beliefs are essentially uncertain, contestable, unproved or unfounded. That is the basic premise of the whole theory, which follows from acceptance of the alleged divorce of fact from value, description from prescription, metaphysics from ethics. Thus education has become fundamentally problematic, and explicitly so, as with hindsight we see that it must be upon the new cosmology and anthropology. The taken–for–granted right and duty authoritatively to

teach has been lost. It is now a *problem* as to what, if anything, can be honestly taught.

2. The positive content of Rational Autonomy is an attempt to solve this problem with the injunction that the young are to be taught to make up their own minds on these matters, and not to have them made up for them by parents or teachers. The young are thus to determine their own fundamental beliefs and thus their way of life.

3. Professor Dearden, in particular, apparently extends the promotion of rational autonomy to all beliefs and judgments, and all the principles upon which they are based, all of which the child is to learn critically to assess and accept or reject. And Mr Wilson has indicated that the young are to be enabled to be, in effect, their own metaphysicians and to work out their own religious or non-religious views for themselves, while Dr Barrow has recommended that they be taught about the two basic types of world-view, 'scientific' and 'religious', so as to promote tolerance [6].

4. But, while the young are to be taught to determine themselves and be autonomous, they are also to be taught to do this *rationally*, to make up their minds on the basis of critical thinking. They are not to be *merely trained* but to be *educated*: viz. to be taught to 'justify' and 'rationalise' their judgments and beliefs, to 'clarify their values', and even, according to Dearden, the principles and criteria used in forming them. The content of education will be heavily intellectual and academic, a position taken generally by contemporary philosophy of education, which virtually identifies the person with 'rational mind', as Hirst describes the 'centre of the child's being' [7], and education with the promotion of knowledge and understanding.

5. Equally, they are not to be left to be supposedly autonomous and self-determining as they are, for then they would not be *rationally* autonomous, and perhaps would not be autonomous or self-determining anyway but under the influence of others.

6. Therefore while the ultimate aim is autonomy, teachers must exercise direction, compulsion and authority upon and over the young in the meantime and in their state of comparative ignorance, to bring them to that goal of rational autonomy. As especially argued by Professors Peters and Hirst, such an exercise of authority is necessary but also temporary, in aiming to enable the young as adults to live without authority [8]. And Mr White was concerned to keep compulsion in schooling to a necessary minimum [9]. Hence the theorists of rational autonomy reject child-centred theory which claims not to direct the child, and also its subjectivism in waiting upon the child's private 'needs and interests', and likewise De-Schooling proposals to make the young the arbiters of what they are to learn, when, where and how [10]. Such views assume that children are already autonomous, or capable of being autonomous, and put no value on rationality. Conversely, Radical theorists attack this defence of temporary authority, direction and compulsion as not being really liberal, while R. Young stands somewhere between them and many Rational Autonomists in arguing that children are capable of greater rational autonomy than Peters, for example, would allow. But the theorists of Rational Autonomy equally reject traditional forms of education in which a specific and substantive content is authoritatively taught, at least in matters moral, political and religious. That is, according to Hirst, a 'primitive' conception of education.

7. Education thus has a positive task and content. What is to be taught above all is those general principles of moral and other types of reasoning, or Forms of Knowledge (Hirst), or processes of clarifying values, or exercises to move them on finally to the stage of autononomous moral thinking (Kohlberg), which will enable the young rationally to form their own judgments and beliefs and so not accept any on authority. In addition, some theorists, notably White and Barrow in their extensive developments of a curriculum (which converge to a high degree even though White starts from a Libertarian position and Barrow from a Utilitarian one), add such ancillary items as bodies of information about contemporary society, alternative ways of living (from history and fiction), ways and means, obstacles and problems social

and psychological, and generally useful skills. Mr Wilson in his writings has also stressed habits and emotional dispositions requisite for rationality and autonomy. The theory of Rational Autonomy thus would endorse, and be a cause of, the shift in schools to the teaching of of the methods, rather than the specific contents, of science, history and geography.

8. Hence there is a tendency to advocate neutrality with regard to substantive matters, except where the theorists are confident about their truth, as with the general principles, Forms of Knowledge, bodies of empirical fact, which they would have taught and whose possession will also aid rational autonomy and associated dispositions such as 'open-mindedness' and 'critical thinking'.

Implicitly, or explicitly as by Hirst in *Moral Education in a Secular Society*, this theory claims to be metaphysically neutral, not to be based on a world-view, and not to teach any. Rather, as with the new RS, which presents museums of 'world religions' or 'stances for living' for the young to look at, or cafeterias of the same wherein they may taste and swallow or eject as they please, teachers should neutrally teach the historical and geographical facts *about* them (who has believed and done what, where and when), or, in addition, promote a critical attitude towards them.

But, as suggested above, this theory does rest upon and embody a definite world-view and in its practical implementation it would impart it. For self-definition, in terms of fundamental beliefs, is its explicit goal for education. It therefore assumes that man does not have a fixed nature but is totally open [11], and that there is no Law or Way outside of him according to which he can and should conduct himself. On the contrary, the young are to be taught to make up their own. Moreover, if there were a Law, Way or *Tao* present in the world, then we could *know* it; we could *correct* and not merely change our beliefs about it; we could definitely be *right* or *wrong* about it, nearer to or further from it; and we all, parents and children, teachers and pupils, would be duty bound to recognize and follow it to the best of our abilities. It would be *authoritative* over us, and we, as responsible parents and adults, would be responsible to it and for the response of the young to it, for bringing them to know, respect, cherish and follow it. We would have the right, rather the duty, *authoritatively* to teach it to the young, to bring them up within it and, as all traditional educational practice and theory has assumed, to

> Train up a child in the Way he should go:
> And when he is old, he will not depart from it (Prov. 22:6).

Conscience, a word not found in contemporary Analytic moral philosophy and the theory of moral education based on it, would come to the fore, as the individual's awareness of that Law or Way. And his proper up-bringing would include the development and strengthening of conscience, the voice of the Law. But, since no ideas like these are to be found in contemporary theory, and, on the contrary, all the stress is upon the making up of their own minds by the young, albeit rationally, one can only conclude that that theory rests upon a denial of the existence of such a Law, Way or *Tao*, and that therefore it rests upon the alternative cosmology and anthropology of man as a self-defining subject in a meaningless universe. In particular, it embodies or is a Liberal Individualist version of that cosmology, one which sees each man as making up his own mind, although White favours participatory democracy in all or most institutions and organisations, and thus, to a certain extent, interprets rational autonomy also in collectivist terms.

The cosmology implicit in the theory of Rational Autonomy presupposes an ontology of the world as mere fact devoid of value-qualities and, because it assumes that we each are to make up our own minds about the ways we are to follow, it also presupposes that there is no Law, Way or *Tao* present in the world under which we all stand. Hirst followed the usual interpretation of G.E. Moore's rejection of Naturalism [12]. Now Moore held goodness to be a simple and unanalysable quality like yellow, but, unlike yellow, to be a 'non-natural' one, one not apprehended by any of the senses. It is a quality which is found simply to adhere to things such as works of art and friendships. Analytic philosophers after Moore gave up the notion of a non-natural quality, and so assumed Reality to be merely factual and lacking value-qualities. Moral judgments were then taken, by the Logical Positivists, to be nonsense, for they were not statement of fact, assumed to be necessarily bare and neutral, nor could they be necessary truths, for the latter were taken to be only tautologies and statements of moral principle are clearly not like 'All bachelors are unmarried'. Thus they were interpreted as mere exclamations of feeling (Ayer) or as attempts to arouse feelings in others (Stevenson). The task for Analytic philosophy then became that of saving what one could from the demolition of ethics, but without giving up the ontology of Positivism which equates Reality with neutral fact. In that task Professor Hare has taken the leading role, and his work, or the tendency of which he is the foremost representative, has been followed by the theorists of Rational Autonomy, of whom he is also one. Hare acknowledges that, as a consequence of the rejection of 'Naturalism' (i.e of *any* connection between fact and value), 'we are free to form our own moral opinions in a much stronger sense than we are free to form our own opinions as to what the facts are' [13]. He then seeks a limitation on that freedom by insisting on universalisability. Hare interprets moral utterances, not as exclamations, but as prescriptions, commands addressed to oneself or others yet, unlike mere commands, intended as binding on all similar persons in similar situations. He is careful to point out that this is a merely formal and logical requirement, and is not the same as the substantive moral principles that all persons should be treated alike and that one should not make exceptions in one's own favour. Those principles he endorses separately and in terms of the Utilitarian generalisation of interests [14]. He thus explicitly adds a Utilitarian content to the Kantian (or, rather, quasi-Kantian) form. In this he is closely followed by Hirst, while Barrow explicitly advocates a Utilitarian ethics and view of life and education. Likewise Kohlberg acknowledges that his final stage of moral development is one of Kantian formalism (but, again, without the beliefs in Pure Practical Reason and its ability to deduce a concrete content from the mere form alone).

While, then, to its proponents and to many of their readers the theory seems to be mere common sense in the pedigree of Locke, Hume, Bentham and the Mills, a deeper grasp of its assumptions reveals that it too manifests some features of modern Gnosticism. For it is explicitly a theory of salvation by *knowledge, gnosis*. Not, of course, the speculative mythology of original Gnosticism, but the academic knowledge in Hirst's Forms or as prescribed by Barrow and White, and, more importantly, the enlightenment, to be implicitly communicated, that *one has been 'indoctrinated'* (by parents, other teachers, society generally) and now is to be saved from 'indoctrination' by being enabled rationally and critically to choose for oneself. It thereby also shows itself to be Gnostic in its sense of alienation, and in the implicit transmission of that sense of alienation to the young, from the society in which its proponents and recipients have been brought up, from the customary and accepted beliefs and practices around them, and in the consequent wish to determine all such matters for oneself [15].

I have previously published criticisms of the following aspects of Rational Autonomy:
1. The claim that methods can be taught without the use and the teaching of substantive judgments and beliefs [16].
2. The claim that we can avoid 'indoctrination' in the several meanings given to that term or the several procedures which are condemned as 'indoctrinatory' [17].
3. The claim that Rational Autonomy promotes political freedom. Rather, I argued, it would destroy society and freedom with it [18].
4. The claims that the exercise of authority in education is only temporary and that education can teach the young to live without authority [19].

5. The claim that the theory is one of *rational* autonomy in the first place. Rather, I pointed out [2∅], it is precisely upon those matters which the theorists regard as having no rational basis – religious (or other) world-views, moral and political beliefs – that they prescribe that the young should make up their own minds. And, in contrast, where the theorists think that matters have a rational basis – Forms of Knowledge, principles of moral and other reasoning, useful information, emotional dispositions that promote discussion and reflection – then they have no hesitation in prescribing them for the young, and do not agonise over allowing or not allowing the young to make up their own minds about them. The theory is thus really, and on its own terms, one of *irrational* autonomy.

I shall not rehearse here my arguments in support of those criticisms. In addition, I have just argued that the theory is, and cannot, be metaphysically neutral, and there are four other criticisms I would also make:

1. That the effective implementation of the theory would require a totalitarian state which could take the young away from the 'indoctrinatory' influences of their parents and other adults. The young would then be 'de-doctrinated' of any moral, metaphysical or political beliefs which had been implanted in them, and would then be kept in a morally, metaphysically and politically neutral environment until they could be taught to reason out their own beliefs

2. That such a policy would be impossible in any case, since men necessarily have moral, metaphysical and political beliefs, which they explicitly or implicitly present to each other, and thereby influence each other's corresponding beliefs, one way or another.

3. That the theory is self-contradictory in inferring that, because *nothing* can be known or rationally affirmed about substantive moral questions (because the world is a collection of bare and neutral facts from which no prescriptions can be inferred), that *therefore* we *ought* to promote rational autonomy in the young. That is as substantive a moral prescription as any, and therefore, on the assumptions of the theory itself, quite without foundation [21]. Moreover, as such it should not be 'imposed' upon the young, or, in other words, they should not be 'indoctrinated' with it. Yet it is to be the basis of their education, and so they are to be implicitly and explicitly taught that they should be rationally autonomous. Likewise Values Clarification implicitly teaches that its processes of freely choosing, clarifying, prizing, standing by and acting upon one's own values are themselves *unquestionably* valuable [22].

5. Consequently, the theory and all the practices which presuppose it necessarily contradict themselves in authoritatively prescribing some substantive moral and metaphysical beliefs while claiming not to do so. *In education there is no neutrality.* For in setting anything before the young for them to learn, or at least to listen to, we are necessarily implying that what we thus set forth is, in one way or another, good, right, true and important, and that what we do not set forth is thereby either not so good, so right, so true or so important, or is definitely bad, wrong, erroneous or trivial.

That the empty self which is rationally to determine itself is an incoherent notion, in and by itself, and doubly so when it is supposed to determine itself rationally. Sartre has presented such a view of the self in his *Being and Nothingness*, and to him we now turn.

Sartre's *Being and Nothingness* is the clearest and fullest articulation of the modern view of man as radical freedom in its Individualist version. Of course, Sartre went on to espouse Marxism and to try to base it on Existentialist foundations in his *Critique of Dialectical Reason*. Therein he manifested that shift from radical Individualism to radical Collectivism which we have seen in Rousseau. Sartre was inspired by Heidegger's *Being and Time*, or, rather, by one side of that work: viz. the account of man as *Dasein*, 'thrown' into the world, living inauthentically in the idle chatter of the 'they' and so forgetful of Being, but still prone to *angst.* Sartre rejected some parts of Heidegger's account: for example, authentic existence as 'living towards death'. Moreover, Heidegger returned from this excursus upon *Dasein* ('being-there') to his prime concern with *Sein* ('Being'). Though Being remains elusive and unspecifiable, it is clear in Heidegger's later works that man is not radically autonomous and self-defining but has a cosmic role to play in relation to it: viz. to be open to it, to respond in conscience to its call, to speak for it [23]. Heidegger rejects European metaphysics from Plato onwards, for forgetting Being in a preoccupation with beings, but, instead of embracing the modern cosmology, returns in several respects to the pre-Socratic philosophers.

In *Being and Nothingness* Sartre operates with a fundamental distinction, taken from Hegel, between being-in-itself and being-for-itself. The former is the solid and fully determinate being of things, whereas the latter is the being that is consciousness. Sartre holds that consciousness, as well as being consciousness of something, is also and always consciousness of consciousness, i.e. self-consciousness. He distinguishes between the non-thetic or non-positional form of (self-)consciousness, which we may gloss as that implicit and alongside awareness which we have of what we are doing and of what is happening to us, and the thetic or positional form, which is the reflective making explicit of the former. He appears to assume that there are no limits upon the latter, and that one can be fully aware of oneself. That is presupposed by the theory of Rational Autonomy which would have each of us choose what he is to believe, be and do. And it is also presupposed in Sartre's account of human freedom. But if, as Polanyi and others have argued, there is always a tacit dimension to all our knowing which can never be rendered wholly explicit, then we never can be fully aware of ourselves. And since you cannot choose what you don't know, in such a case we can never choose and determine all that we are, think and do.

Consciousness is also 'nothingness', a hole in being, as is shown, Sartre claims, in the experience of vertigo. In vertigo I become vividly aware that *nothing* compels me to save my life nor to prevent myself from hurling myself into the abyss. What is then revealed to me is the extent of my freedom, the freedom which I, as consciousness, am. *Nothing* separates me from my past. I *am not* my past. In anguish I become fully aware of this, that I do not have to do and so can do anything. Thus the reformed gambler, faced once more with the gambling tables, sees in anguish his resolutions melt away as he realises that nothing stops him from gambling again (pp.28-33). Mostly we live on the level of non-thetic or implicit (self-) consciousness, and so we go along in our accustomed grooves. In Bad Faith we try to convince ourselves that we *must* do what we usually do or what others expect of us, and in particular that we *are* our social roles. We thus try to hide our radical freedom from ourselves in order not to be anguished by it. But in order to hide it, we have to know it. Bad faith therefore suppresses and so implies the nothingness which we *are* in relation to ourselves (p.44). This nothingness of the self Sartre elaborates throughout the book in relation to the fundamental dimensions of man's being, such as his past, present and future, and his relation to himself and to others. It is summed up in the oft repeated formula that 'consciousness is not what it is and is what it is not'. That means that I cannot be identified with any state of myself nor any action that I perform. What I *am* is always my past, that is, what I *am not now.* Thus if I say that I *am* a lecturer that can mean only that I *have been* one, for *nothing* stops me from giving it up at this moment. Equally, as a consciousness agent trying to realise various projects (e.g. to finish this book) I am what I *am not yet* (the author of this completed work). I do not have and cannot have the being-itself which simply *is,* except when when I am dead and my existence is wholly congealed into the past.

We cannot now follow up the ramifications of Sartre's account of man as nothingness. In any case what matters for us is that it is presupposed by the idea of man as self-determining subjectivity. To determine myself throughout I must be *nothing* to begin with. Thus there cannot be a determinate human nature nor a determinate individual essence. We noted Hirst's explicit denial of a human nature, and now with Sartre we are beginning to see what that implies.

Furthermore, to be radically self-determining I must choose for myself, as Dearden has seen, the fundamental principles by which I choose. They cannot be *given* to me, for then I would be at bottom determined by them and not myself. I may not create my own values but I must choose them. Again, Sartre spells out what this really implies. Values cannot be founded on *being*, he argues, for then they would not be values (but merely neutral facts, being-in-itself) and would result in heteronomy of the will. Rather, they are revealed only to an active freedom which makes them exist by recognising them as such, i.e. which chooses them to be its values. My freedom is the unique basis of values, and, of course, *nothing* justifies me in adopting any one value or scale of values. The explicit recognition of this causes anguish, for my choice of my values cannot itself have any foundation (p.38). (Nietzsche wanted this recognition to result in joy.) Again, in Bad Faith we hide our free choice of our values from ourselves and claim that in some way – by God, Nature or Society – they are given to us. Sartre thus makes it clear that only my *arbitary* choice can make any values values for me. The project of Rational Autonomy rests on a fundamental self-contradiction. For if I am to determine *everything*, then, as Dearden rightly said, I must choose my canons, standards, criteria, principles and values whereby I am to choose everything else. But Dearden has also repudiated Sartre's insistence on arbitary choice. Yet if that choice is not to be arbitary I must have further principles, and so on, whereby I choose my principles, values and the like, and which are therefore given to me and not chosen by me.

Sartre therefore reveals the project of human life as an absurdity. We cannot make the avoidance of Bad Faith and thus the achievement of sincerity our aim, for to do that is contitute oneself as sincere *in order not to be it*. That is, in making sincerity my aim, I claim to be sincere but thereby am not yet sincere since I make it my aim to be sincere. I can be sincere only about what I am: that is, my past, what I have been. For I am essentially nothing. To be what I claim to be I would have to attain the being which is being-in-itself, the fully determinate being of things, which are just what they are. But as consciousness I can never be that. Thus I can only *play* at fulfilling a role, at experiencing an emotion, at *being* anything (pp.59–63).

One might object that here, and in other places, Sartre is eliding distinctions which can clearly be drawn in life, and that there are paradigmatic examples of good faith which cannot be gainsaid. But that would be to miss the point. For, while it is true in terms of our ordinary view of ourselves as having an essence (yet not a wholly fixed and determinate one), such a view of man is repudiated by Sartre at the outset and, by implication, by the theory of Rational Autonomy. Given the opposite assumption, that man has no essence and is nothingness, then he never can coincide with himself and will always transcend what he is at any instant. If we are what we choose to be, as Sartre insists and as Rational Autonomy would have us be, then in ourselves we are nothing except this perpetual activity of choosing. This nothingness which we are Sartre also expresses as 'a lack' and as 'a being such that its being is in question'. We are not things but freedom, radical freedom.

While we are each nothingness in ourselves, we do have a 'being for Others', the structures of which Sartre elaborates in detail. It must suffice for us to note that I am not and transcend what I am for another. The Other has a determinate view of me, as possessing certain characteristic, habits, mannerisms, desires, and so on. But this is necessarily an alienation of myself, for really I am none of these things. The Other inevitably objectifies me and makes me 'a transcendence transcended'. We cannot know each other as subjects, for as subjects we are *nothing*. We therefore see each other as, or rather as seeing each other turn each other into, objects in the world and as instruments or obstacles to our projects. Unlike Marxist and other Gnostic alienations, which are phases of human history or episodes in the cosmic drama, this alienation is fundamental and can never be overcome. Here, as elsewhere, Sartre's logic is, in substance, inexorable though it may be stretched and forced in some of its detail. The empty self which is what it chooses to be is not anything determinate and so cannot be known. All that can be known is the determinate being that I have been. Therefore, if we are like this, then there can be no meeting of minds, no common projects, no communion. The 'we', Sartre rightly argues on his premises, is a secondary and derivative phenomenon, which arises from the anonymous persons for whom devices and procedures are intended--the anonymous anyone to whom 'Exit' and 'Entrance' are addressed and which apply to me and you as possible visitors. The experience of 'we' is thus an event in my mind alone and a way of feeling myself among others, as one of the stream of passengers leaving or entering the station via the passages marked 'Exit' and 'Entrance'. Thus such objects and experiences presuppose the orginal experience of the Other, the one who looks at me and thereby fixes me as a determinate being, the object of his gaze (pp.425–8).

It follows therefore that all human desires and projects are doomed to frustration for they aim at what is self–contradictory. This Sartre reveals, in the chapter on 'Concrete Relations with Others', in respect of our relations with others wherein what we want is to possess each other as free subjects. But the nothingness that is the Other cannot be grasped. Fundamentally, what man wants is *to be*;he is '*the desire to be*'; and that means to be simultaneously a being–for–itself (consciousness, freedom) and a being–in–itself, to be the 'in–itself–for–itself' which is God (p.565). But freedom cannot have any essence, and for man 'existence precedes and commands essence' (p.438). I *am* and do not *have* my freedom. I am condemned

> to exist forever beyond my essence, beyond the causes and motives of my act. I am condemned to be free.....we are not free to cease being free (p.439).

Therefore each human being is a 'passion', an unrealisable desire that brings suffering, because we aim to lose ourselves, to *be* and to be something definite, to escape 'nothingness', and so to achieve 'the In–Itself which escapes contingency by being its own foundation, the *Ens causa sui*, which religions call God'. Hence we aim to accomplish the reverse of the work of Christ, to lose ourselves as men in order to give birth to God. 'But the idea of God is contradictory and we lose ourselves in vain. Man is a useless passion' (p.615).

Sartre concluded *Being and Nothingness* with some reflections on ethics. Parallel to G.E. Moore, he affirmed both that no ethics could be deduced from ontology but that ontology could show what sort of ethics would be possible. Since ontology has shown (rather Sartre has assumed throughout) that values have no basis in being, the serious attitude, which takes them to be real and independent of our choice, is to be repudiated (p.626). Thus, it seems, what is possible is the contrasting attitude of play, wherein one makesone's freedom manifest (pp.58Ø-1) (Compare Nietzsche's joyful creation of values.) And Sartre ends by wondering if freedom can make itself its own value and should choose as its ideal being–what–it–is–not and not–being– what–it–is: that is, to accept the limitations of our humanity and not try to be God.

In the lecture *Existentialism and Humanism* he sought to carry through that possibility. He restated the main doctrines of *Being and Nothingness* and then set up freedom as its own ideal. Agreeing with Kant that universalisability (applying precepts to all) is the form of moral principles, he rightly rejected Kant's attempt to deduce a content from the form. The content, he insisted, is always concrete and unpredictable, and so he repudiated all general rules (pp.52-3). He proposed freedom as its own end, on the gounds that, when someones has seen that he chooses his values, 'in that state of forsakenness he can will only one thing, and that is freedom as the foundation of all values' (p.51). He further argued that in willing our own freedom we will that of all others. For while my freedom, as my essence, does not depend on others, once in 'total authenticity' I recognise that we all, as men, cannot but will our own freedom, I then also simultaneously recognise that I necessarily will the freedom of others (p.52). What he tried to do, then, was to give a humanitarian and libertarian prescription for the use of our freedom. This, as Hare saw, was parallel to what Hare himself wished to do on similar grounds.

But Sartre later repudiated that lecture and realised that his prescriptions therein were quite arbitary. Here, again, his logic was better than that of our Analytic philosophers. For, if values are my free projection, then there is nothing to stop me from, just as there as nothing to justify me in, preferring to live in Bad Faith and the serious attitude, or to will my freedom and not that of others, or to do anything else. Similarly, on Hare's assumptions there is nothing at all to justify his prescribing Utilitarianism filling for his Kantian form nor to stop anyone else from prescribing other things. *If there are no values in Reality itself, then everything is a matter of arbitary choice.*

Apart from the arbitariness of the basic prescription, Sartre's project was doomed on its own terms. For in *Being and Nothingness* he had rightly concluded, on his own assumptions, that we cannot promote the freedom of other. Since the Other is also a 'nothingness', I cannot apprehend him. To grasp him as this or that, is to fix my idea of him upon him, to make him something determinate, to objectify him. Therefore even if I try to follow Kant and make the Other's freedom and 'end in itself', I thereby 'transcend his transcendence' and make an object of the 'nothingness' that is his radical freedom. Equally, if I seek to benefit him, I thereby use him, the 'Other-as-object', in realising my goal of realising his freedom. I see him as a thing, an instrument, in a situation which I intend to alter as I also intend to alter him. (After all, he may not want to be free and may wish to go on in Bad Faith in his usual roles.) 'Thus I am brought to that paradox which is the perilous reef of all liberal politics and which Rousseau has defined in a single word: I must "force" the Other to be free' (pp.4Ø8-9). Since the Other is nothing in himself, and since there are no values other than what I arbitrarily choose to take as such, then whatever I do to the Other is necessarily an imposition of my arbitary preferences upon him. Thus, Sartre continues, if I seek to comfort him in his distress, I arbitrarily set up his freedom from grief as an end for him and organise him as a system of means to that end. (He may wish to enjoy his sorrow.) Nor can an ethics of *laisser-faire*, a policy of non-interference, escape this dilemma. For simply by existing along with him, I set factual limits, necessarily arbitrary, to him and his projects. (E.g. by living next door to him I prevent him from having someone else for a neighbour or playing the trumpet at three o'clock in the morning, *and there is no common good which would not be arbitrarily imposed on either me or him*). Even the attitude of tolerance is (in principle) an arbitary imposition, and would cause him 'to be thrown forcefully into a tolerant world', and thus to remove from him on principle 'those free possibilities of courageous resistance, of perseverance, of self-assertion which he would have had the opportunity to develop in a world of intolerance' (p.4Ø9).

Then come Sartre's brief but very significant remarks on education, wherein he states that both 'a severe education', which treats the child as an instrument in forcibly trying to get him to adhere to values which he has not chosen, and also 'a liberal education', which uses other means, neverthless choose '*a priori* principles and values in the name of which the child will be trained. To train the child by persuasion and gentleness is no less to compel him' (p.4Ø9) (i.e. to 'indoctrinate' him). As before, it is irrelevant to protest that compulsion and persuasion are quite different, or are so at least in some cases. For, if we are as Sartre and Rational Autonomy say we are or should be, free creators of ourselves in a world devoid of values, then whatever we do to the child represents our arbitrary choices which, of necessity, are impositions upon his radical freedom, his nothingness of being. As we saw above, the policy of Rational Autonomy logically requires 'forcing to be free' in the removal of the child from 'indoctrinatory' influences in order to prepare him for autonomy. But, since there are no values in the world on that hypothesis and so no possibility of a common good, then that is an act as arbitrary as any other. *Ex hypothesi* there is nothing bad in leaving children to be 'indoctrinated' and unautonomous, nor good in liberating them from 'indoctrination' and making them autonomous. Indeed, any teaching or influencing them cannot but be 'indoctrination', the imposition of our arbitrary choices upon them.

That is the irresolvable dilemma of the education of autonomous man, who lacks any essence which, even if he had one, would be just another meaningless fact and of no moral significance [24]. On its assumptions we cannot but be arbitrary definers of ourselves who, while we have any contact with the young, impose our arbitrary choices upon them. Sartre has spelt out in detail the inevitably of this dilemma, whereas Nietzsche rejoiced in asserting it, and the theorists of Rational Autonomy fail to carry through the logic of their assumptions. It remains for us to consider one other version of this result, the unconditioned conditioner of others.

But before we do that let us note that it is only within these last twenty or so years that there have been drawn out the full implications of the new cosmology and anthropology with regard to education. The question naturally arises as to why it should have taken so long. In Chapter 1, some suggestions were made about this: the sheer inertia of history, such that men continue to do what they have been accustomed to do, even though it contradicts their new beliefs; and specific reasons in the case of particular theorists. We have noted some of the later with regard to Kant and Hegel. Hegel also represents a partial reaction against the new view of the world and the man, and explicitly sought to reconcile men to the world, especially the social and cultural world around them. A more thorough-going reaction we found in Froebel, but, for other reasons, there is less emphasis in his work than in Hegel's upon the assimiliation by the child of the cultural and social worlds. Yet, because the child is seen as fundamentally already made, and made by God, education is not for Froebel a radical problem. The child's destiny is to express the divine spirit within him and pervading the world. The task of education is negatively not to interfere with nor to inhibit this, and positively to encourage it, strengthen it and make it explicit. Other theorists, such as the Utilitarians and Marx, have tried to restore a positive content to man, life and education, viz. pleasure or unalienated production. Again, education ceases thereby to be a fundamental problem.

The principal difference, it seems to me, is the explicit and widespread adoption of scepticism and relativism with regard to good and duty. That is not new. But in the past it was confined only to a few philosophers such as Hume, who locked away his speculations as unprofitable. The rest of the population, educated and uneducated alike, continued in the firm belief of mankind throughout the ages that some things at least are definitely good or bad and are known to be so. Whatever may be the further reasons for the undermining of that conviction, that fact is that which makes the difference today. Formal education has definitely been one of the further causes: implicitly and explicitly, in schools, colleges and universities, the young are taught that there is no substance in good and right. And thus their education undermines itself and leaves them with no sure marks by which to chart their way through life.

Notes

1. In substance, though not always in name, the following set forth the basic theses of Rational Autonomy, and some develop it in more detail:

   K. Baier: 'Moral autonomy as an aim of moral education' in G. Langford and D.J. O'Connor (eds), *New Essays in the Philosophy of Education*;

   R. Barrow: *Commonsense and the Curriculum*, which is written from an explicitly Utilitarian position;

   R. Barrow and R. Woods: *Introduction to Philosophy of Education*;

   B. Crittenden, 'Autonomy as an Aim of Education' in *Ethics and Educational Policy*, ed. K.A. Strike and K. Egan.

   R. Dearden: 'Autonomy and Education' in Dearden et al. *Education and the Development of Reason*;

   R. Dearden, E. Telfer and R.M. Hare: Symposium on 'Autonomy as an Educational Ideal' in S.C. Brown (ed), *Philosophers Discuss Education*;

   P.H. Hirst: *Moral Education in a Secular Society*;

   J.P. White: *Towards a Compulsory Curriculum* and *The Aims of Education Restated*;

   J. Wilson: *Introduction to Moral Education* and *Education in Religion and the Emotions.*

   Mention should also be made of the moral philosophy of R.M. Hare, who has also written several papers on philosophy of education (for details see the Bibliography in *Moral Thinking*) applying that philosophy, which underlies the theory of Rational Autonomy.

   The theory is also implicit in discussions of 'indoctrination' and also of RE, which, it is always assumed, must be 'indoctrination' if it is the teaching of any substantive beliefs and practices. See virtually all the volumes of the *JPE.*

2. The Schools' Council & The Nuffield Foundation, *The Humanities Project: An Introduction.* For a discussion of some aspects of this proposal by C. Bailey and J. Elliott, see *Proc. Philosophy of Education Society* (now *JPE*), Vol. VII No. 1, Jan. 1973

3. See L. Raths, M. Harmin, and S. Simon, *Values and Teaching: Working with Values in the Classroom.* In Values Clarification what matters is the process, not the outcome. The process has seven aspects: Choosing (1) freely, (2) from alternatives, (3) after consideration of their consequences; Prizing (4) being happy with the choice, (5) willing to affirm the choice publicly; Acting (6) according to the choice, (7) repeatedly in a pattern of life. Many schemes of work implementing this proposal have been published and used in American schools. A useful summary of Values Clarification and samples of criticism of it, along with similar summaries and criticisms of Kohlberg's approach, are to be found in, ed. D. Purpel and K. Ryan, *Moral Education.*

4. Kohlberg's scheme has been set out and developed in many articles, several of which are to be found in his *Collected Papers on Moral Development and Moral Education.* His stages are: I. Preconventional Level: 1. orientated to avoiding punishment and obedience to power; 2. orientated to statisfying one's own and sometimes others' needs; II Conventional Level: 3. 'good boy--nice girl', orientated to conduct which pleases or helps others and is approved by them; 4. orientated to law, order, doing one's duty, showing respect for authority; III Post-conventional, autonomous, or principled level: 5. orientated to general rights of individuals, free agreement and contract as binding obligations; 6. self-chosen, abstract, comprehensive moral principles (e.g. the Golden Rule, the Categorical Imperative) and not determinate laws as in the Decalogue. Any survey of what people are supposed to think finds out only answers to the questions asked. One sees in Stage 5 the Liberal Individualist version of the new cosmology, which we noted in Hobbes, Locke, and one level of Hegel, and in

Stage 6 a semi-Kantian Formalism. Had Kohlberg approached his subjects in other terms, e.g. Natural Law, different 'stages' would have resulted.

5. 'Metaphysics in Education', *JPE*, Vol.23 No. 2.
6. Wilson, *Education in Religion and the Emotions*; Barrow, *Commonsense and the Curriculum*, pp.13∅-6. On p.51 Barrow characterises the 'scientific interpretative attitude' (not science itself) as that in which life is seen as a whole as being in man's own hands for him to make what he will of it. This, of course, is not the *scientific* world-view but that of man as self-defining subject in a meaningless universe. The religious one is there defined as that which involves mystery, undemonstrable axioms and man as subject to a law or destiny. And that, of course, is not necessarily a religious world-view but, in its last element, defines any traditional cosmology. Peversely, he cites Hegelianism and Marxism as examples of the 'religious' attitude. But neither saw man as subject to any external law or destiny, Marx was militantly atheist, both denied mystery, and Hegel claimed that his philosophy was totally transparent and proved and therefore 'science'.
7. *Knowledge and the Curriculum*, p.28.
8. See Peters, *Authority, Responsibility and Education* and Hirst and Peters, *The Logic of Education*, pp.114-23.
9. *Towards a Compulsory Curriculum*
1∅. See R. Barrow, *Radical Education.*
11. As explicitly stated by Hirst, *Moral Education in a Secular Society*, p.29.
12. *Moral Education in a Secular Society*, p.3∅.
13. *Freedom and Reason*, p.2.
14. *Freedom and Reason*, p.118.
15. It is interesting that Barrow and Woods (op. cit. p.3) endorse the Existentialist notion of 'inauthentic existence' (Heidegger's 'Fallenness') as a state out of which philosophy should rescue us. They discount its 'portentous theological overtones', which, in fact, represent the Gnostic kinship of the idea.
16. 'Religion, Emotion and Education', *JPE* Vol. 3, No. 2;
17. 'The Philosophy of Michael Polanyi and its Significance for Education',*JPE*, Vol. 12, 1978.
18. 'Rational Autonomy: the Destruction of Freedom', *JPE*, Vol. 16, No. 2, 1982;
19. '"Because I Say So!" Some Limitations on the Rationalisation of Authority', *JPE*, Vol. 21, No. 1, 1987.
2∅. 'Rational Autonomy....'
21. See R.F. Atkinson, 'Instruction and Indoctrination' in R. Archambault (ed), *Philosophical Analysis and Education*, who, it seems, rightly concludes that there can be no distinction between 'indoctrination' (bad) and 'education' (good) within Analytic moral philosophy and its denial of objective values. But, it appears, no one has taken any notice of this.
22. For this and other penetrating criticisms of the advocates of Values Clarification, especially their failure in the second edition of *Values and Teaching* to address previous criticisms, and for useful references to those discussions, see D. Boyd and D. Bogdan, '"Something" Clarified, Nothing of "Value": A Rhetorical Critique of Values Clarification', *Educational Theory*, Vol. 34, No. 3, Summer 1984.
23. See Heidegger on man's role as 'the Shepherd of Being' in his 'Letter on Humanism', a reply to Sartre's *Existentialism and Humanism.*
24. Hare, *Freedom and Reason* p.122, states: 'The duties which we acknowledge towards people are not derived from the "essence of man" or from any philosophical mystification of that sort; they are acknowledged because we say, "There, but for good fortune go I"'. Precisely! There is nothing right or wrong in itself, on his assumptions, in rape, theft, slavery, murder or any other indignity perpetrated on men's humanity, for there is no such thing nor any

values and disvalues in anything at all. And so we are left with the mere fact, bare and neutral, that 'we' don't do some things because we would not like them done to us. Hare's bases his ethics upon this fact, a manifest return of 'Naturalism' by the back door after it has been ostentatiously ejected via the front. But if, as Hare states, there are not nor cannot be values in things themselves, then we are left with merely neutral facts and thus with no ethics or a necessarily 'Naturalistic' one.

8 Helvetius and Skinner: The unconditioned conditioners

In these studies we are concerned with the belief in man's autonomy or radical freedom consequent upon the belief that the world is merely a mechanical system of things in space and time and therefore without meaning. Another consequence of the latter belief is the assumption that man is also just another part of that system and to be understood in similar terms. As we have seen with Kant, these two consequences, seemingly contradictory of each other, are not so opposed to each other as one might at first think. Furthermore, the empty, or nearly empty self, is also an assumption of the various Reductionist psychologies – from Hobbes, through Locke, the French Sensationalists, the British Associationists to contemporary Behaviourism – which hold either with Locke that the mind or self is originally nothing but a *tabula rasa* or with the Behaviourists that it inherits a set of unconditioned reflexes. (I except those Reductionist psychologies, like McDougall's, and those of the socio-biologists, such as E.O.Wilson, which hold the self to be wholly determined by genetic endowment.) In the former case, what the self becomes is wholly a matter of how it is affected by circumstances, and, in the latter, of how those innate and unconditioned reflexes are turned by circumstances into a more numerous and complex set of conditioned ones. And those sociologists who assume the self to be the product of its social conditioning, the dimensionless point at which various roles intersect, and so object vehemently to any ideas of genetic endowment, and not just to the exaggerations and fancies of the socio-biologists, differ from Behaviourists only in holding that the empty self is filled by its social relations.

We shall now study the conjunction of man as radically free and man as totally determined in the contrast between the Behaviourist's explicit view of all men, and certainly of others, as wholly determined and conditioned beings, and his tacit view of himself as the free and unconditioned conditioner of others.

Now there is another contrast between those who stress the determination of man by circumstances, social or natural or both, and those who stress the determination of man by genetic endowment: viz. the belief of the former that therefore man's future, individually and collectively, is open, since he can be whatever circumstances make him, and the belief of the latter that man's possibilities, individually and collectively, are fixed, totally or within a narrow range by his genetic inheritance. Hence the hostility shown by Marxists and Marxisant sociologists to all expressions of belief in genetic limitations which they regard as a 'reactionary' view. Consequently, usually accompanying the idea of the self as a nothingness, or next to nothingness, which is then determined and filled by circumstances, is a belief in human progress, often infinite progress. For, it is argued, if the circumstances, material or social or both, are changed in appropriate ways, so then will be human life.

We have already met one version of this combination of ideas in Marx. There it is also joined with an apocalyptic view of history and a definite immanentization of the End, at the beginning of which pre-history stops and real history (but without any great drama) begins. But it has been more often accompanied by beliefs in progress which envisage no exact End to and within history nor one to be achieved by Revolution, and which stress continued amelioration and reform, of the sort that Marx condemned. But there may well be a belief in a dawn which has come or is at hand, an age of enlightenment, when reform will get under way and lead men out of the darkness and misery of the past and present. For, as was remarked before, in history things never return to just where they were before, and if people lose the Christian hope of the vision of God in eternal life, they do not return to paganism. What we shall be concerned with is thus the view or views of education formed within a belief in continued human progress and reform, in this life and in this world, as the result of accumulating changes in those circumstances, natural or social or both, which make men what they happen to be at any given moment, while there is no transcendent Law or Way for men to follow nor moral order within the world itself.

The belief in human progress through the transformation of Nature, is often dated from Francis Bacon. But Bacon is notably ambiguous. On the one hand, with Galileo, Hobbes, Descartes and Spinoza, he is one of the originators of the naturalistic view of the universe as a mechanical system of particles of matter in motion, and thinks that there is one inductive logic which applies to all sciences. On the other, he affirms both natural and revealed theology, and does not give any naturalistic account of man, as does Hobbes, nor explicitly separates him from Nature as free subjectivity, as does Descartes. Yet he holds that the value of knowledge is 'the benefit and use and men', 'the relief of man's estate' [1], i.e. the improvement of man's physical conditions in the universe. In that respect, he is rightly held to be originators of the Utilitarian view of education.

We find in the French Sensationalists the link between aspirations for human progress, in intramundane terms, and a naturalistic and determinist view of man. Misreading Locke, they omitted his 'ideas of reflection', and so made the mind into nothing but a concatenation of 'sensations'. Hence whereas Locke had said (at the beginning of the *Thoughts on Education*) that nine tenths of what a man is, he is because of education, Helvetius concluded that a man is wholly a product of his education (i.e. of all the influences upon him of his circumstances to date) and therefore that education (as so understood) can do everything. Education, in the ordinary as well as in Helvetius' very wide sense, therefore becomes a potent instrument in the reshaping of man's condition and thus of man himself.

Unfortunately for our purposes, the works of Helvetius are not readily accessible [2]. But he does clearly present the complex of ideas now under consideration and apply them himself to education. And in his work we can see the transition from an account of man as orientated to a good and law beyond himself to one of man as a mechanism of pleasure and pain within a purely mundane context. In contrast, we find in Bentham that account merely taken for granted. And as Bentham's views of education have already been studied by Professor Bantock, I shall present a summary of Helvetius' theories of man and education, although I shall have to use secondary sources for *De l'Homme*. We shall then turn to a contemporary representative of the same general outlook, Professor B.F.Skinner who does try to deal with some of the key questions which arise with regard to it, questions which, so far as I know, Helvetius did not face.

Helvetius makes clear the manipulative intentions of the new psychology: 'To guide the motions of the human puppet it is necessary to know the wires by which he is moved'. And, 'To educate, furnish their minds and render them happy we must know to what instruction and what happiness they are susceptible' [3]. Now Plato had used the same image of man as a puppet but a puppet which is the plaything of the gods, and who should be controlled – i.e. control himself – by the 'golden string' that links him to the right reason enshrined in the law of a well-constituted state (*Laws* 645a), a law that itself is modelled on the transcendent Good. In contrast, Helvetius has no transcendent reference. He is usually thought to have been a Hedonist and to have held man to be driven by desire for pleasure and aversion to pain. But, argues Voegelin [4], for Helvetius the fundamental forces within man are *paresse* or inertia, and those which counter-act this: viz. ennui, the inequietude which drives men to find minor pleasures in the intervals between stronger ones, and the passions which drive men into actions which incur fatigue. The last produce great men, great actions and great achievements. Helvetius then supplies a genealogy of passions, which may be schematised thus:

physical sensibility→ love of pleasure and hatred of pain→ *amour de soi*→desire for happiness → desire for power → the 'factitious' passions (envy, avarice and ambition) which are the means of obtaining power.

Now whereas Nietzsche, as we saw, did take the desire for power to be fundamental in man and so regarded Helvetius as the last great event in morals, Helvetius himself, while wanting to show it as the basic force which in varying circumstances takes such forms as avarice and ambition, tried also to derive it from a sensationalist psychology which makes pleasure and pain fundamental. But, as Voegelin remarks, he makes no attempt to explain what pleasure is procured by facing death. Voegelin draws attention to the presence in Helvetius' scheme of the *amour de soi*, which is St Augustine's *amor sui*. But in the Christian anthropology that is what prevents man from realising his creaturely finitude, his dependence on God. What we note is that now it has been been given a purely mundane reference. It ought to be synonymous with the desire for power, but, argues Voegelin, Helvetius continues its negative tones from Christian thought, and sees it as that orientation to one's own good which deflects men from promoting the general interest [5]. Helvetius here introduces a moral note into his mechanistic psychology. It thus opens the possibility of manipulating man, by the legislator and educator, in accordance with some supposedly real standard of value. And Helvetius regards the *amour de soi*, and all that comes after it, as acquired. 'One learns to love oneself; to be human or inhuman, virtuous or vicious. Moral man is altogether education and imitation' [6].

But the great problem for Hedonists has always been to explain (a) what is really *good* about pleasure, and (b) how the individual seeking pleasure – *his own* pleasure – can come to seek *as good and as a duty* that others feel pleasure as well. For if pleasure is the only good, I cannot take pleasure in something *because it is good*, and I can only like, be indifferent to or dislike what I meet, just as I happen to feel. And so I can only happen to like, be indifferent to or dislike the sight and thought of others enjoying themselves or suffering. You cannot tell me that I *ought* to like their enjoyment and dislike their suffering, because these are, respectively, good and evil. For, if pleasure is the only good and pain the only evil, then, if I like to see them suffer, dislike them enjoying themselves, or am indifferent to both or either, these things are, respectively good and bad, or either or both is neutral, as far as I am concerned, and there can be no *ought* about it. But Helvetius is reported as making no effort to explain the transition from pleasure-pain to good-evil.

Voegelin, calling attention to the incredibility of supposing that Alexander and Caesar acted out of calculations of pleasure and pain, explains Helvetius' preference for Hedonism (over the more convincing idea of the desire for power) in terms of a correct perception of the drives animating the men of his time – the French court of the eighteenth century – which is wrongly taken to be the universal truth about man. This, comments Voegelin, is a 'willingness to mistake the abuse for the essence in order to continue the abuse, with the best of surface intentions, for a different purpose' [7], viz. to serve as the basis for a manipulative technology whereby men's desires and feelings, and thence their actions, can be shaped, by law and education, so as to promote the greatest happiness of the greatest number, the formula which Helvetius originated. Voegelin further comments that Helvetius' analysis is 'a classical instance of the destruction of the integral human person by positing as normal the disorder of the person while denying to man the remedial powers which might restore the order'. And, instead, the function of regeneration is transferred from God to the pschologist turned legislator who brings about those social situations which, by operating on the mechanisms of human minds, will make men's conduct conform externally to moral standards. Men are emptied of moral substance and placed under the control of the analyst–legislator. 'Mankind is split into the mass of pleasure–pain mechanisms and the One who will manipulate the mechanisms for the good of society' [8].

I would add that, within the purely mundane framework with which Helvetius thinks, there can be no objective *ordo amoris* to set the standard for human desires and emotions, for what, as Plato said (*Laws* 653b) is rightly to be loved and rightly to be hated. There can only be the facts that men, all or some, love this and hate that. So, then, what is to guide the Great Manipulator? He, too, is part of the mechanism of pleasure and pain, or tacitly exempts himself from it. In the former case, he can manipulate the rest only for *his* pleasure and to avoid his own pain, *whatever they may be*. It may coincide with what pleases others, or it may not. But, in this framework he has no freedom to will otherwise. And, if he does tacitly exempt himself from the determinism which he applies to others, then there is no real good, Law or Way to guide him, and he implicitly sees himself as Sartrean man, an undetermined nothingness, condemned to choose, but with no rational means of choice. So, once again in accordance with Hegel's dialectic, we swing back to the contrary position, and again the unconditioned conditioner, being a for–itself and radical freedom, is like the conditioned, the in–itself, in being able to act only as he pleases and following what he merely happens to like or dislike. In Nietzsche's terms, the free manipulator is thus implicitly a self–appointed overman who not only creates (or chooses) values for the herd to follow but who also, with his 'behavioural sciences', conditions them into conduct coinciding with those values.

As far as I know, Helvetius never raised these questions, but, like Bentham after him, simply assumed the legitimacy of the greatest happiness (in terms of material comfort) of the greatest number, for which, of course, he could have no warrant. As we shall see, Professor Skinner has risen to this challenge. But before turning to his approach to man and education, let us briefly see how Helvetius conceived of the tasks, nature and methods of education upon these assumptions.

The differences among men, such as that between geniuses and the rest, are the result of education in the wide sense: of the differences in the governments under which they live, the circles in which they are born, the educations which they receive, the desires they have of distinguishing themselves, and the ideas to which they attend. The art of education is thus that of placing young people in the circumstances in which their minds and virtues can be developed [9]. Its power, then, is very great. Education is thus 'the art of forming men' (in a very strong sense for men are almost nothing in themselves) in order to form 'stronger and more robust bodies, more enlightened minds and more virtuous souls' [10]. These last are innocuous sentiments and everything depends upon the precise sense given to the

64

terms used. As we have seen, there is no real place for virtue in Helvetius' psychology but only for habits which give pleasure to self and others. Likewise the enlightenment of the mind can mean only a clearer grasp of means to pleasure. But Helvetius passes over these problems and asserts that the general aim of education is 'to render men more happy and generally useful to their country' [11]. That is, 'The one certain point that the principles of education ought to regard is the greatest public utility; that is the greatest pleasure and the greatest happiness of the largest number of citizens' [12].

What education needs specifically to do is to store the memory with ideas and to arouse the strong passions (to overcome lassitude) [13]. Education will also include a significant amount of physical training to render the individual fit and healthy, for his sake and that of others, and this is to be enforced by law. Similarly, since pleasure is the sole good and because therefore (Helvetius assumed) ignorance is the cause of wrong action, the mind must be given appropriate information: viz. that value arises from the sensitivity to pleasure and pain, and that society and its institutions, laws and customs have arisen from the pursuit of happiness by individuals. In turn that requires a moral catechism for judging the utility of actions, a calculus of pleasures and pains produced. And the passions are to be strengthened so that men act on what they have been taught. In particular, the love for glory and esteem are to be re-inforced since these are the drives that lead to actions of general benefit.

As well as what applies to all, Helvetius requires attention to be paid to the likely occupation of the individual and to what is specifically required for it, so that his memory can be stored with appropriate ideas and objects. Any other procedure is absurd.

Formal education for all will thereby promote social progress: by spreading knowledge and enlightenment so that men will not be ruled by ignorance, fanaticism and intolerance; by actualising in more and more people the potentialities for genius; and by diffusing knowledge of what is good and how it is to be achieved, so that men will be more inclined than now to seek their own and each other's greater pleasure.

The content of education is, of course, to be determined by considerations of utility within this world and this life. Thus there will be only the national language, except for those few who can master Latin and Greek. For Latin has no merits as a general discipline whereby industriousness and application may be acquired. Natural sciences will be included, both for their technological benefits and for the changes which they produce in attitudes to man and society. Likewise the social sciences. Subjects such as literature and art, and those parts of natural science without technological application, are included in so far as they are intrinsically pleasant, that is, as found to be so by contemporary taste.

His conceptions of method derive from his Sensationalist psychology, and refer to the activity of the teacher, since the pupils, having no passions, are passive in learning. Thus he stresses clarity in presentation, simplicity of language, and movement from simple to complex and from particular to general, and frequent repetition: that is, the teaching of discrete items one by one. As for the driving forces within the pupils, these, of course, are feelings and calculations of pleasure and pain, which are to be changed, inhibited or re-inforced by making the content pleasant intrinsically or extrinsically (with rewards), by showing it to lead to pleasure later on, and by playing on the love of glory in order to arouse socially useful traits of character.

Given Helvetius' belief in the power of education, both in the ordinary and the very wide sense, he naturally favours a uniform system, and thus the ending of schools run by religious orders, the aims and content of which he logically rejects in any case. All education is to be organised by the state, so that it can be directed to a coherent end. So too must it be provided in schools and away from the influence of parents: 'In general, that education is best where the child is most distant from his parents, has the least opportunity of mixing incoherent ideas with those he ought to acquire in the course of his studies' [14]. Here we have a clear statement of the totalitarian view of education, which is so embedded in the modern view of man that it is implicit, as we saw in the previous chapter, even in those who claim to be Liberals. Voegelin quotes, as showing the influence of Helvetius, a telling passage from an introduction, approved by Bentham, to a contemporary French translation of his work. It states that, if there could be found a way of controlling all the influences upon a given number of people, so that one could mould them exactly as one wished, then such a method 'would be a very powerful and a very useful instrument which governments might apply to various objects of the utmost importance' [15]. And, in a footnote on the same page, Voegelin continues the quotation from the French. The author adds that education is no more than the result of all the circumstances in which the child is placed. Consequently, to manage someone's education is to manage all his actions, and to put him in a position where one can influence him as one will by choosing the objects that will form his ideas. In view of such a passage, we see how superficial can be the distinctions usually drawn between Liberalism and Collectivism. As Voegelin comments, these sentiments were also those of the Gestapo and Lenin. Both pose the same questions: *Who* is to control these powers and influences, and to *what* ends? – *especially when man has to choose his own ends and values or when some will choose them for the rest.*

We now turn to B.F.Skinner for a contemporary version of the same complex of ideas [16]. Skinner's Behaviourism is the culmination of the great dream of applying the methods of modern science to man himself. Skinner is quite explicit about this and what it entails: that behaviour has no 'peculiar properties which require unique methods or special kinds of knowledge' (*SHB* p.36); that we cannot apply the methods of science 'to a subject-matter which is assumed to move about capriciously'; that the use of the methods of science requires that 'behaviour is lawful and determined'; that 'we shall discover' that a person's actions result from specifiable conditions; and that 'once these conditions have been discovered, we can anticipate and to some extent determine his actions' (*SHB* p.6). It is not that we shall *discover* that action is determined by antecedent conditions, but that a Reductionist view of man must assume that it is. And we note the clear expression, in the final clause, of the manipulative hopes behind that assumption.

The realisation of those hopes is the message of his *Beyond Freedom and Dignity*, which is a sustained polemic, indeed a diatribe, against the idea of autonomous man, that is, man as possessing free-will, the power of choice and initiative. Autonomy, as free-will and choice, is an invocation of the miraculous to explain what we cannot yet explain otherwise. It is, Skinner implies, an obscurantist tactic to prevent the development and application of a science and technology of human conduct. He therefore seeks to debunk the notions of human freedom and dignity which stand in the way of that development. The whole book is a work of prophecy: a call to apply the science of behaviour, which Skinner assumes the doctrine of operant conditioning to be, as a technology by means of which to cure the ills of civilisation and to further the progress of evolution.

We need to make vast changes in human behaviour, and we cannot make them with the help of nothing more than physics or biology (*BFD* p.4).

A technology of behaviour is available which would more successfully reduce the aversive consequences of behaviour, proximate or deferred, and maximise the achievements of which the human organism is capable (*BFD* p.125).

The intentional design of a culture and the control of human behaviour it implies are essential if the human species is to continue to develop (*BFD* p.175).

This is the same totalitarian dream as that of Helvetius, Bentham, Nietzsche, Hitler and Lenin, except that the first two would have the maximisation of pleasure as the end, Nietzsche the creation of new values and their acceptance by the herd, Hitler the survival and mastery of the Aryan race, and Lenin the production of Socialist Man.

Again, education, in the ordinary as well as the very wide sense, is a part of this technological fantasy. We see that in Chapter XXVI of Skinner's *Science and Human Behaviour*. There education is conceived in terms of operant conditioning and the use of artificial reinforcers, such as stars and grades and promises of entry into jobs or controlling élites, to produce specific objectives themselves characterised in terms of specific pieces of behaviour, such as restating a text or performing a set of discrete and defined actions. The details of Skinner's Behaviourist view of education do not now concern us, for our interest is in his conception of it as part of the grand machinery for remaking man and society and the question of the ends which it is to serve.

To the last we now turn. What, in a world of 'objective facts', mechanical causes and operant conditioning, can be good and right? Skinner answers in terms of reinforcers, positive ones which promote the reperformance of a piece of behaviour. A judgment of value is one about how someone feels about a fact and therefore about its reinforcing effect (*BFD* p.1Ø4). That is, 'I think X is good' means 'I like X' and in turn 'Doing X will make me do it again'. But, of course, thinking to be good is not the same as liking (one can dislike or be indifferent to what one regards as good) and liking is not the same as doing again (one can decide not to repeat something which one liked). And we judge the goodness of things which have nothing to do with us, our likings and our actions, such as actions, people and events in the past. None of this can be admitted into Skinner's vision of man. For Behaviourist man does not, nor cannot act, because of reasons, beliefs and judgments in the first place, since these are all mythological notions used to hide ignorance of the real causes of behaviour: that is, of the antecedent events which have conditioned the relevant reflexes. Thus a person 'does not act for the good of others because of a feeling of belongingness or refuse to act because of feelings of alienation. His behaviour depends upon the control exerted by the social environment' (*BFD* p.11Ø). Considerations of good and evil are therefore irrelevant, or, rather, non-existent. *They are judgments which human organisms **cannot** make.*

But, of course, Skinner himself *does* make them and writes his book to persuade us to agree with them and to work towards realising them. But he has to camouflage them as statements of mere fact, of facts about behaviour. Thus 'You ought to tell the truth' he takes to mean 'If you are reinforced by the approval of your fellow men, you will be reinforced when you tell the truth' (*BFD* p.112). He has never heard of knowing (or being told) what one ought to do yet not doing it. So, then, with what set of mere facts does he camouflage his own valuations and prescriptions? With those of 'survival'. I shall present and comment upon his argument (*BFD* p.144):

(1) He states that a culture, 'which *for any reason* induces its members to work for its survival' is more likely to survive.

Note the unBehaviourist personification of 'culture' which renders an abstract term into a name for an intelligent being. Note also the collectivism implied therein, and expressly stated in the next sentence.

(2)   This is 'a matter of the good of the culture, not of the individual'.

But what can Skinner mean by 'the good of a culture'? Only what reinforces it, but to do what? To survive, presumably, but a reinforcer is such only as producing repeated behaviour, and 'reinforcing a culture' signifies nothing about just what it is being reinforced to do, given that it can be said to 'do' anything in the first place. For example, it could just as well refer to producing repetitions of behaviour which bring on its demise.

(3) Deliberate design can promote 'the good of a culture' by 'accelerating the evolutionary process, and since a science and technology of behaviour make for better design, they are important "mutations" in the evolution of a culture'.

But what is 'the evolutionary process'? If Skinner intends this as a piece of biology, he can refer only to changes which bring about the emergence *or disappearance* of new species. Evolution is neutral as regards direction and value. If design accelerates it, it accelerates only in the direction in which it is already going: survival, change of form *or extinction*.

Again, note the collectivist and totalitarian assumptions behind the notion of designing a culture: *Who, whom?*, as Lenin would have said.

(4) 'If there is any purpose or direction in the evolution of a culture, it has to do with bringing people under the control of more and more of the consequences of behaviour'

'If there is any purpose': in a Behaviourist world there cannot be any purposes in anything. These are precisely the mentalist obfuscations that Skinner wants to eliminate from the language. And, apart from that, there cannot be purpose or direction in it unless it is supplied by God from without or by an immanent *Geist* from within.

Note again, in the last sentence, the tyranny of the whole (and of its designers) over the parts. Note there also the standard Behaviourist fallacy of invoking explanations in terms of *future* events, 'consequences', which, of course, cannot affect anything, where what is really meant, but cannot be said, is people's or animals' *expectations* or *beliefs about* the consequences of their actions.

But why should Skinner write such crass nonsense? It is because his Behaviourist assumptions do not permit him to speak explicitly of values and choice, yet there are clearly things which he does regard as valuable and which he wishes us to choose. Thus in Chapter 8 of the same work he expresses his disapproval both of what is happening to children and of the way in which the problem is currently conceived. In contrast, he proposes *better* ways of bringing them up. But, in his language, 'better' can mean only 'more effective', and he wants to say more than that: viz. to endorse an end towards which the more effective means (of operant conditioning) are to be applied. Thus on the one hand he explicitly states that his technology of conditioning is 'ethically neutral' and can be used by villains as well as saints. (But how can he, on his assumptions, speak of 'villains' and 'saints'?) And, on the other, he wants it to be used for the *improvement* of the human lot, and goes on to say that we are concerned here, 'not merely with practices, but with the design of a whole culture, and the survival of a culture then emerges as a special kind of value' (*BFD* p.15∅). But it does nothing of the kind. It does not 'emerge' but is *chosen* by Skinner as a special of value – that is, given that he can consistently talk of values in the first place. He tries to dodge acknowledgment of his act of choosing by discounting other options as merely arbitrary and subjective preferences. Thus he says that an individualist, 'will design a world in which he will be under minimal control and will accept his own own personal goods as the ultimate values'. Another, exposed to a different conditioning, will design 'for the good of others, possibly with a loss of personal goods'. (Yet what can Skinner mean by the *good* of others?) In contrast, 'If he is concerned primarily with survival value, he will design a culture with an eye to whether it will work or not' (*BFD* p.151). That is, Skinner is trying to argue that others would impose arbitary preferences, whereas he, 'concerned primarily with survival value', is looking only to a neutral effectiveness. But this both hides his choice of *survival* as the end, and ignores the fact that everyone else will be concerned with making his scheme work: effectiveness is no monopoly of survivalists.

Of course, what Skinner should say is that people do not choose anything at all, but merely act according to the way in which their reflexes have been conditioned, so that those who get into positions of designing cultures will design them as they have been conditioned so to do, and that he himself does not choose but does, or would do, what he has been conditioned to do. But no one applies, nor can coherently apply, determinism to himself. Consequently, the truth of the matter, which he cannot say, is that he himself is the unconditioned conditioner who imposes his arbitary preferences, his chosen values, on others. Nietzsche made that very clear, but Skinner's Behaviourism prevents him from stating what he is doing.

Yet he does face the question, raised by C.S.Lewis in *The Abolition of Man*, of what, in the absence of any Natural Law or transcendent Way, those who rule are to choose to impose on the rest. For, as Lewis rightly argued, if there is no such Law or Way, then there can be no education, no imparting of the *truth* which can be freely recognised and accepted as such. Instead, there can be only an of arbitary choice of what is to be imparted, on the one hand, and its imparting by way of conditioning on the other. Thus 'the power of Man to make himself what he pleases means.....the power of some men to make others what *they* please' [17]. Nietzsche happily and Sartre regretfully agree, and see no other possibility, since God is dead, while the theorists of Rational Autonomy, whose assumptions entail the same conclusion, accuse everyone else of drawing it and try to avoid it themselves. Yet Skinner logically ought to disgree only on the grounds that 'the autonomous agent....is replaced by the environment' (*BFD* p.184), so that, in the proper sense, no one *does* anything, and instead we are like wires through which currents run or like billiard balls through which a force is transmitted from the one before to the one after. Now he does rejoice in the abolition of 'autonomous man'--man with the power to choose--and his replacement by what is 'manipulable' (*BFD* pp.2ØØ-1). And he says that: 'Man himself may be controlled by his environment'. But, since no one can really believe that he himself lacks all choice and initiative, Skinner immediately tries to have it both ways and adds, 'but it is an environment which is almost wholly of his own making' (*BFD* p.2Ø5). He asserts that the same self is both controlling and controlled, conditioning and conditioned. This is true, within his assumptions, just as one billard ball both is hit and hits. So, in a sense, we collectively make each other, or would do so if we had no power of choice. But Skinner does not believe that of himself, yet will not admit it, and so will not admit that he has arbitrarily chosen 'the survival of a culture' as the end to which he proposes that some of us shall effectively condition the rest. And, of course, that is precisely what would happen, or what some – those who hold or seize power, who believe themselves to be unconstrained by any moral law which they have not chosen, and so who have only their own arbitary preferences to guide them – would try to do to the rest of us.

Here then, we have the tacitly empty self, not only arbitrarily determining itself, but, armed with a technology for manipulating others, seeking explicitly to determine others according to its necessarily arbitary choices. It is only in the explicitness of its aims with regard to the young that Skinner's view of education really differs from that of Rational Autonomy. From such a state of affairs – the self-destruction of radically autonomous and self-defining man – only recognition of and adherence to the Law or Way can deliver us.

> Either we are rational spirit obliged for ever to obey the absolute values of the *Tao*, or else we are mere nature to be kneaded and cut into new shapes for the pleasures of masters who must, by hypothesis, have no motive but their own 'natural' impulses. Only the *Tao* provides a common human law of action which can over-arch rulers and ruled alike. A dogmatic belief in objective value is necessary to the very idea of a rule which is not tyranny or an obedience which is not slavery [18].

And, we may add, it is just as necessary to an education that is not arbitrary manipulation.

Notes

1. *The Advancement of Learning*, Bk I, V 11.
2. Principally *De l'Esprit* (1758) (hereafter *E*) and *De l'Homme* (1772, posthumously).
3. Quoted Grossman, *The Philosophy of Helvetius*, p.78.
4. *From Enlightenment to Revolution*, p.43ff.
5. Compare Rousseau's account where it is also negatively evaluated.
6. Quoted Voegelin, op.cit., p.48 from *De l'Homme*.
7. ibid. p.5Ø.
8. ibid. pp.5Ø-1.
9. *E*, pp. 37Ø-1.
1Ø. *E*, p.492.
11. Grossman, p.127.
12. idem. What follows is taken from Grossman and refers mostly to *De l'Homme*.
13. *E*, p.492.
14. Grossman, p.143.
15. Voegelin, op.cit., p.6Ø.
16. References to Skinner's works will be given in the text using the following abbreviations:
    BFD = Beyond Freedom and Dignity
    SHB = Science and Human Behaviour
17. *The Abolition of Man*, p.37.
18. ibid. p.44.

9 Conclusion

In the last three chapters we have seen the final appearance of what the new view of man in the world means in respect of education. Nietzsche, Sartre and Skinner, the latter despite himself, show us that when man has no superior Law or Way to which he is responsible, then the education of the young can be only the imposition upon them of our arbitary, unfounded and unjustified choices. The theorists of Rational Autonomy, holding these same assumptions, attempt to avoid the consequences by claiming to have a formula for a rationality that is a matter of form alone, and not one of content and substance: viz. a matter of imparting methods whereby the young can then rationally form their own opinions and beliefs for themselves. I shall not repeat here the arguments which I have presented elsewhere against that possibility. Instead I shall only point out once more that, apart from such considerations, the project is doomed in any case because *all* notions of good and duty are held to be matters of arbitary choice, and thus so must be the opinion that the young *should* be taught to be autonomous. Even if there were a rational form and set of methods which could be separated from particular contents, that would still leave any content, any actual opinions about what we should or should not do, as arbitary and unjustified as they were before. If, then, we accept the basic assumptions of the modern view, what then should we do?

In one sense, there is no problem, for we are free to do just as we like and any who would gainsay us are merely expressing their own private and unfounded opinions. We can choose Rational Autonomy, the breeding of higher man and the Overman, conditioning to promote 'the survival of a culture', the promotion of the classless society, the dominance of the Aryan race, or anything else whatsoever. All are as equally unjustified as each other. And if we think that some possibilities are *not* to be chosen or that one or more others *should* be chosen, then either we hold this to be merely our own arbitary preferences or we have in effect abandoned the modern view and implicitly hold there to be, somewhere and some how, a superior Law or Way which is *not* a matter of our choice but which summons and commands us by its own intrinsic authority. It is therefore really pointless to weigh up the

71

comparative merits and demerits of those prescriptions for education which unambiguously embody the modern view. They can have genuine merits and demerits only on the assumption that their own fundamental premises are false, and that things can have real values and disvalues which we do not project arbitarily upon them. And to take that position is to have abandoned all of them at the start. Nevertheless, since no one ever actually is an outright 'immoralist' – certainly not Nietzsche himself – and always reserves some things which, despite his own explicit statements of principle, he holds to be really right and good or wrong and bad, there may be a point in appealing to that lingering belief by pointing to particular weaknesses in each theory.

Firstly the type of theory most clearly represented by Skinner, the adherents of which do not see that they do not, nor cannot, apply their theories to themselves. No one can treat himself as a wholly conditioned thing and not as a responsible person. Once that is explicitly acknowledged, then the position in question changes to one essentially akin to Nietzsche's: the explicit proposal that one, or some, shall arbitarily choose or invent values and goals for the rest to follow, and that the rest shall be so manipulated that they do in fact follow them. The converse of $n-1$ conditioning is the position adopted by the theorists of Rational Autonomy, who explicitly predicate freedom to all but who, on their own premises and despite their intentions and claims, implicitly reserve the right to impose their unfounded preferences upon others. Once the real implications of their assumptions are realised, their position again becomes fundamentally the same as that either of Nietzsche (some choosing for the rest) or of Sartre (each choosing for himself but without any pretensions to rationality).

Now the positions of Sartre and Nietzsche have at least the merits of realising that arbitary and unjustified choice is the consequence of the assumptions which they hold and of explicitly accepting it. Nietzsche's theory of education has the additional merit of recognising the facts of human inequality and the need for commanding and obeying. Even if the programme of Rational Autonomy were logically coherent, the intellectual demands which it makes – for extensive reflection, self–scrutiny, logical analysis, abstract operations – in order to think out critically one's own beliefs, obviously put it beyond the abilities of most of the young and most adults as well [1]. What Rational Autonomy in practice comes to, and must come to, is something like Nietzsche's explicit prescription: viz. that some – the intellectually and socially dominant, the articulate and fluent – will end up choosing their own values, principles, beliefs, and so forth, and imposing them upon the rest. And the theorists are committed to doing that themselves in any case. But Nietzsche's specific programme cannot be carried through because no one has, nor can, invent any new values but can only extoll one or more old ones and denigrate others, just as Nietzsche did himself.

Where, then, do we go from there? Sartre would argue that that is where we are stuck, in the perpetually frustrated desires *to be* and to enjoy the other as freedom. If man is a nothingness that defines himself, then Sartre is right. All we can do is go through those circles of one frustration after another, which he elaborates in 'Concrete Relations with Others', and through others like them.

Two apparent ways out are offered by Helvetius (and the other Utilitarians, and by some of the theorists of Rational Autonomy) and Marx, both of which represent a retreat from the assumption of the empty self. On the one hand, men are assumed to be creatures of pleasure and pain, and, on the other, to be essentially producers, especially of things. If either is correct, then surely we have a definite and non-arbitary content for life and education. As for the Utilitarian thesis, pleasure is nothing in itself: it is essentially pleasure in doing this or that. And if pleasure is the only good and end, then all pleasures, as Bentham held, are equal, and there can be no relative evaluation of them except in his terms of intensity, duration, fecundity and compatibility. That is what Nietzsche clearly saw in his terms of will to power, strength and life. Thus, as we saw, he emphatically repudiated any notions of equality among men, for men manifestly differ in capacity for will to power. And they also differ in capacities for pleasure. Bentham's maxim, endorsed by Hare [2], that each is to count for one and for no more than one, is, firstly a totally arbitrary assumption in any case (as are all moral principles on Bentham's and Hare's presuppositions) and flatly contradicted by the different capacities which men have for pleasure and pain: the sensitive feel more of both than do the insensitive. And we cannot in any case rule out any pleasures, such as those of the Sadist, for, *ex hypothesi*, pleasure is the only good and so no pleasure can be bad since there is no principle on which it could be evaluated as bad. If there is a greater balance of pleasure over pain when one man tortures another than when he doesn't, then that is the way things are and *should be.*

What, then, about Marx's view of man? It does give an aim to life, but it does not resolve the basic problem. Men are producers, but of what? Instruments of torture and amusement, of food for eating and beer for drinking? We saw how Marx repudiated vulgar enjoyments (parallel to Matthew Arnold's distaste for the 'populace' and its 'fun'), but, without some real order of values and higher Law or Way, that can be only his private opinion. What it has amounted to in fact is that curious Socialist obsession with production for its own sake (especially production of capital goods), neglect of services, and distain for what consumers actually want. It amounts, in the end, to a collectivist form of Utilitarianism. Moreover, Marx's view has other problems, notably the logical impossibility of its End and the tyranny of the future over the present. The former problem is also that of Rousseau and of all attempts to overcome the limitations upon individual self-definition by substituting for it a collective self-determination, wherein we all are jointly to negotiate what we shall all do, so that the resulting pattern of life will reflect the will of each of us. Such a programme is impossible, not only because of the pragmatic difficulties presented by assembling everyone together and getting free agreement from diverse and often perverse people, some of whom will want to do the opposite of whatever it is that the rest agree upon, but also because of the logical impossibilities of (a) getting free agreement when, *ex hypothesi*, there is no real order of values or superior Law which all can recognise and accept as a common standard, and (b) negotiating *everything from scratch* and without any initial conditions and fixed points, which, of course, would thereby *not* be the products of the participants' wills. It would be like trying to navigate in a totally uniform and featureless desert under an equally blank sky. The latter problem is that of all systems which 'immanentize the eschaton', which bring the End of history into this world as a future state for men on earth. When that is done, the present is nothing but the means of getting to the End, whatever it is, *and so are all men alive at the present.* Hence the ruthless use of everything and everyone by the revolutionary totalitarian such as Lenin, who, acting strictly by the logic of his position, treated everyone around him as strictly disposable means to bringing in first the Revolution and then the dictatorship of the proletariat (i.e. of the Party) in order finally to bring in the classless society. Robespierre likewise tried to execute the logic of Rousseau's totalitarian democracy. And Nietzsche would have his higher men use the herd, and other higher men, in order to bring in the Overman. Those living before the End are viewed as Skinner views everyone, as 'beyond freedom and dignity'.

Can we find a non-arbitrary way of determining ourselves, and thus of educating the young, within the modern view of the world? That is the fundamental problem which the systems under review have so far failed to answer. What about Kant's system? He certainly claimed to have found a rational and logically necessarily formula for human good and duty, based on the form of a rational will and not upon any order of values or transcendent Law, a formula which he futher thought to coincide with traditional notions of what we should do. Hence he had no real difficulty in outlining an appropriate and largely conventional scheme of education.

But, as has been often pointed out, Kant's system is fatally flawed. All that the Categorical Imperative can tell us is what cannot qualify as a principle of human duty, and never what positively we should do. It leaves our duties hanging in the air, empty of content. Thus it can tell us that we cannot have as a principle of duty that others should respect property while I may steal, or that other married persons should remain faithful to their spouses while I commit adultery. But it cannot tell us that property is to be respected in the first place or that sexual relations are to be confined to those who have made vows of fidelity towards each other. Kant simply took such things for granted but on his assumptions these are mere facts and making them principles of duty would be 'heteronomy of the will'. Sartre, for a while, and the theorists of Rational Autonomy, following Hare, have adopted Kant's formalism while rightly, but not fully, admitting that any content they give to it is quite arbitary (on their assumptions). Formalism can get going, as Scheler demonstrated, only when it is acknowledged that there is a real order of values which summon and command us by their own authority and not just as we happen to like them, and which thereby provide the rational and non-arbitary content for the formal system.

And so we come to Hegel. If anyone could provide a way of avoiding the dilemmas of the modern view of man and the world, it was him. As we saw, he sought to stabilise the situation, the fuller working out of which in terms of the theory of education we have seen in those authors whom we studied afterwards. And he sought to do that by locating self-definition, not upon the individual self nor even upon human collectivities, having realised that both of these are impossible in theory and massively destructive in practice, but upon a cosmic yet wholly immanent *Geist*, whose process of self-definition is human history. If the modern world-view can be interpreted in such a way that it is logically coherent as a theory, logically possible as a policy, and social and politically stable when executed and lived by, then Hegel's version is the one required. In it meaning and purpose are restored to human life; man is reconciled to the world; the individual is reconciled to the society and age in which he finds himself; and a coherent policy for the education of the young for their places in society and the world is outlined. And should we find that life around is lacking in meaning and coherence after all, then it can be shown to us that this state of affairs is only a transient but necessary 'moment', deeply meaningful and coherent *because of* its surface lack of meaning and coherence, in the cosmic drama of *Geist* defining itself in and through Nature and then man.

But has Hegel succeeded? The answer to that question, as Hegel would tell us himself, is to be found in his *Logic*, which we had to omit, and which we cannot study here. Everything turns upon the logical possibility of an initially empty *Geist* filling itself by its own efforts with a content that is rich and diversified yet rational and non-arbitary. In his *Logic* Hegel claimed to have recovered the logical procession of the general structure of the actual world from the initial starting-point of abstract and empty Being. I, for one, would say that in the end he did not solve the problem but only restated it at great length. For the problem is insoluble: *ex nihilo nihil fit.*

In addition Hegel's system is also one that brings the End, the realisation of Absolute Spirit, into history, and so devalues all stages prior to it as mere preparations for it. It was this aspect of Hegelianism that provoked the protest of Leopold von Ranke: 'Every age is immediate to God and has its significance in itself'. Likewise, despite Hegel's acceptance of the modern notion of the value of the individual person as such and in himself, the World Spirit merely uses individuals and groups as its vehicles in realising itself, and their rights are overridden by its [2].

The idea of self-definition proves incoherent in theory and destructive in practice, whether we locate it in the individual, the group or a cosmic Spirit. In one side of Froebel we met an attempt to regard the self as already made and thus to have as its task the expression of the divine spirit within it. Froebel interpreted that in the traditional terms of Christian Theism, more or less, whereas others held the divine

74

spirit to be wholly within the world. Froebel could not follow his own claim that the child develops outwards from within, and explicitly stated that, at the age of eight, the child must assimilate the world outside him. Child-centred education, having given up Froebel's Theism, tried to see the child's life and development as one wholly of the expression of a self already fixed. But if we are already made, there is no need for nor no possibility of education, just as education is rendered impossible by the idea that the self is wholly empty. Once we grant that we are in the making, the question of which self or which aspects of the self should be expressed, encouraged and developed, necessarily raises itself. And it can be answered rationally and non-arbitarily only if there is some Law or Way for man which we do not invent. Froebel rarely raises that question, for it is not relevant if the child's nature is already determined and determined by God, so that he follows the Law of God automatically.

We are left either with acceptance of Sartre's account of the inexorable frustrations and sheer arbitariness and absurdity of human life, or with a decision to make a complete break with the modern cosmology and anthropology. For the faults which we have found are structural and beyond remedy. Education presupposes what the modern view, in all its variations, does not permit: that man is *responsible*. We can be responsible only insofar as we are both free but not empty, that is, (a) insofar as we have a definite human nature but one that is not closed, and (b) also as we are subject to a Law or Way which we do not create.
(a) Without the former, there is no *person* to be responsible for himself, only a wholly determinate in-itself, determined by external forces, or a wholly indeterminate nothingness. Sartre would accept the fact of empirical constants in human nature, but would insist that we are still free to accept or reject them and that *nothing* justifies us in doing either. And without a Law or Way to tell us what is really good, or bad, in human nature, the desires, traits of character, emotional dispositions and other features of the self which we find within ourselves, are likely to be resented as merely *given* to us and not chosen by us.
(b) Thus it is the lack of a superior Law or Way that is decisive, for such a Law or Way would give us the directions in which our human nature *should* be developed, and that in a rational and non-arbitary manner. Furthermore without it, there is nothing *to* which we can be responsible and by the light of which we can act responsibly.
   Therefore, if there is a non-arbitary Law or Way, binding upon both us and them, which we can bring up the young to obey or to follow, then we have the power to be responsible for ourselves, for them and for bringing them to be responsible for themselves. What the theory of education therefore requires is a doctrine of man, a philosophical anthropology, which acknowledges and articulates the definite human nature – physical, organic, psychological, social and spiritual – which we have and yet which we also have consciously to develop, and with it a philosophical cosmology which locates man in a world wherein he is under a superior Law or Way, which he can freely follow or disobey, and which defines the ideal completion of his nature. Only then will education have a rational and non-arbitary notion of what the young should brought up to be.

Notes

1. Hirst, *Moral Education in a Secular Society*, p.98, states that not all children can become autonomous but does not follow this up, and Kohlberg finds that few progress to Stages 5 and 6.
2. *RH* p.65, 'the individual may well be unjustly treated; but this is a matter of indifference to world history, which uses individuals only as instruments to further its own progress'; pp.69–71 on the monstrous sacrifices of the past

having been made so that today the individual can work for causes to which he freely assents; p.89, 'A mighty figure must trample many an innocent flower underfoot, destroy much that lies in its path'; p. 89, on the inadequacy of particulars to the universal or type, and the consequent sacrifice of individuals. 'The Idea pays the tribute which existence and the transient world exact, but it pays it through the passions of individuals rather than out of its own resources'; p.9∅, 'individuals in general come under the category of means rather than ends'; and p.91 on the fate of individuals as irrelevant to the rational order of the world.

Bibliography

Archambault, R.D. (ed) (1965), **Philosophical Analysis and Education,**
   Routledge, London.
Bantock, G.H. (198∅, 1984), **Studies in the History of Educational Theory,** 2
   Vols, Allen and Unwin, London.
Barrow, R. (1976), **Commonsense and the Curriculum,** Allen and Unwin, London.
   (1978) **Radical Education,** Martin Robertson, London.
Barrow, R. and Woods, R. (2nd ed. 1982) **Introduction to Philosophy of
   Education,** Methuen, London.
Brown, S.C. (1975) (ed) **Philosophers Discuss Education,** Macmillan, London.
Burtt, E.A. (2nd ed. 1964) **Metaphysical Foundations of Modern Science,**
   Routledge, London.
Cohn, N. (1957) **The Pursuit of the Millenium,** Secker and Warburg, London.
Dearden, R.F., Hirst, P.H., and Peters, R.S., (eds) (1972) **Education and the
   Development of Reason,** Routledge, London.
Descartes, R., (1968) **Discourse on Method,** trans. Sutcliffe, F.,
   Penguin, Harmondsworth.
Downie, R., Loudfoot, A. and Telfer, E. (1974) **Education and Personal
   Relations,** Methuen, London.
Froebel, F. (1967) **A Selection from his Writings,** (ed) Lilley, I.M.,
   C.U.P, Cambridge.
Gill, E. (1985) **A Holy Traditional of Working,** (ed) Keeble, B., Allen
   and Unwin, London.
Gordon, P. and White, J. (1979) **Philosophers as Educational Reformers,**
   Routledge, London.
Grene, M. (1969) (ed) **The Anatomy of Knowledge,** University of Massachusetts
   Press, Amherst (Mass).
Grossman, M. **The Philosophy of Helvetius,** Teachers' College, University of
   Columbia, New York.
Hare, R.M. (1952) **The Language of Morals,** Clarendon Press, Oxford.
   (1962) **Freedom and Reason,** Clarendon Press, Oxford.
   (1981) **Moral Thinking,** Clarendon Press, Oxford.

Hegel, G.F.W., (2nd ed. 1892) **Logic,** trans Wallace, W., Clarendon Press, Oxford.
  (1952) **The Philosophy of Right,** trans. Knox, T.M., Clarendon Press, Oxford.
  (1977) **The Phenomenology of Spirit,** trans. Miller, A.V., O.U.P., London.
  (1975) **Reason in History,** trans. Nisbet, H., C.U.P. Cambridge, 1975.
Heidegger, M. (1978) **Being and Time,** trans. Macquarrie, J. and Robinson, E. Blackwell, Oxford.
  (1977) 'Letter on Humanism' in **Basic Writings,** ed. Krell, D., Harper and Row, New York.
Helvetius (1973) **De L'Esprit,** Editions Gerard, Verviers (Belgium).
Hirst, P.H. (1974) **Knowledge and the Curriculum,** Routledge, London.
  (1974) **Moral Education in a Secular Society,** University of London Press, London.
Hirst, P.H., and Peters, R.S. (197∅) **The Logic of Education,** Routledge, London.
Jonas, H. (2nd ed. 1963) **The Gnostic Religion,** Beacon Press, Boston (Mass).
Kant, I. (1929) **Critique of Pure Reason,** Kemp Smith, N., Macmillan, London.
  (1948) **The Moral Law,** trans. Paton, H., Hutchinson, London.
  (195∅) **Prolegomena to Any Future Metaphysics,** trans. Beck, L.W., Bobbs–Merrill, Indianapolis.
  (1956) **Critique of Pure Practical Reason,** trans. Beck, L.W., Bobbs–Merrill, Indianapolis.
  (196∅) **On Education,** trans. Churton, A., University of Michigan Press, Ann Arbor.
  (196∅) **Religion within the Bounds of Pure Reason Alone,** trans. Greene and Hudson, Harper and Row, New York.
Kohlberg, L. (1973) **Collected Papers on Moral Development and Moral Education,** Laboratory of Human Development, Harvard University, Cambridge (Mass).
Langford, G., and O'Connor, D.J., (eds) (1973) **New Essays in the Philosophy of Education,** Routledge, London.
Lawrence, D.H., (1936) **Phoenix,** Heinemann, London.
Lewis, C.S., (1978) **The Abolition of Man,** Collins, Glasgow.
MacIntyre, A., (1981) **After Virtue,** Duckworth, London.
Marx, K. (1963) **Selected Writings in Sociology and Social Philosophy,** ed. Bottomore, T.B. and Rubel, M., Penguin, Harmondsworth.
  (1975) **Early Writings,** trans. Livingstone, R.L. and Berton, G., Penguin, Harmondsworth.
  (1977) **Selected Writings,** ed. McLellan, D., O.U.P., Oxford.
Nietzsche, F. (1954) **The Portable Nietzsche,** trans. Kaufmann, W., Viking Press, New York.
  (1968) **The Will to Power,** trans. Kaufmann and Hollingdale, Vintage Books, New York.
  (1973) **Beyond Good and Evil,** trans. Hollingdale, R.J., Penguin, Harmondsworth.
Nozick, R. (1974) **Anarchy, State and Utopia,** Blackwell, Oxford.
Peters, R.S. (3rd ed. 1973) **Authority, Responsibility and Education,** Allen and Unwin, London.
  (1981) **Essays on Educators,** Allen and Unwin, London.
Purpel, D., and Egan, K., (eds) (1976) **Moral Education,** McCutchan Publishing Corporation, Berkeley (Cal).
Rawls, J. **A Theory of Justice,** Clarendon Press, Oxford.
Rousseau, J–J. (1911) **Emile,** trans Foxley, Dent, London.
  (1953) **Political Writings,** trans. Watkins, F., Nelson, Edinburgh.

Sartre, J-P, (1948) **Existentialism is a Humanism**, trans. Mairet, P., Methuen, London.

(1958) **Being and Nothingness**, trans. Barnes, H.E., Methuen, London.

Scheler, M. (1973) **Formalism in Ethics**, trans. Frings, M.S. and Funk, R.L., Northwestern University Press, Evanston.

The Schools' Council & The Nuffield Foundation, (197∅) **The Humanities Project: An Introduction**, Heinemann Educational Books, London.

Skinner, B.F., (1953) **Science and Human Behaviour**, Free Press, New York.

(1972) **Beyond Freedom and Dignity**, Bantam Books, New York.

Strauss, L. (1953) **Natural Right and History**, University of Chicago Press, Chicago.

Strike, K.A., and Egan, K. (eds) (1978) **Ethics and Educational Policy**, Routledge, London.

Talmon, J.L. (1952) **The Origins of Totalitarian Democracy**, Secker and Warburg, London.

Taylor, C. (1975) **Hegel**, C.U.P., Cambridge.

Voegelin, E. (1952) **The New Science of Politics**, University of Chicago Press, Chicago.

(1968) **Science, Politics, Gnosticism**, Regnery–Gateway, Chicago.

(1975) **From Enlightenment to Revolution**, Duke University Press, Durham (N.C.).

White, J.P. (1973) **Towards a Compulsory Curriculum**, Routledge, London.

(1982) **The Aims of Education Restated**, Allen and Unwin, London.

Wilson, J. (1967) **Introduction to Moral Education**, Penguin, Harmondsworth.

(1971) **Education in Religion and the Emotions**, Heinemann, London.

Young, R. (1989) **A Critical Theory of Education**, Harvester Wheatsheaf, Hemel Hempstead.

Index of names

Adorno, T., 39, 47
Aeschylus, 33
Alexander the Great, 64
Allen, R.T., 7, 59
Aristotle, 37
Arnold, M., 73
Atkinson, R.F., 59
Augustine, 12, 63
Ayer, A.J., 51

Bacon, F., 62
Baier, K., 58
Bailey, C., 58
Bantock, G.H., 1, 2, 22, 62
Barrow, R., 49, 51, 58, 59
Bentham, J., 4, 51, 62, 64, 66, 67, 72–3
Boleyn, Ann, 18
Bogdan, D., 59
Boyd, D., 59
Bosanquet, B., 36
Bradley, F.H., 36
Brunel, I.K., 38
Burke, E., 11

Caesar, J., 43, 44, 64
Castro, F., 5
Clement of Alexandria, 8
Cohn, N., 8
Crittenden, B., 58

Davey, N., 46
Dearden, R., 49, 54, 58

Napoleon, 43, 44
Newton, I., 17
Nietzsche, F., 39, 4∅-6, 54, 55, 63, 64, 69, 71, 72-3
Nozick, R., 8

Peters, R.S., 1, 49
Plato, 13, 53, 63
Polanyi, M., 53

Ranke, L. von, 74
Raths, L., 58
Rawls, J., 8
Robespierre, 5, 1∅, 14, 15, 73
Rousseau, J-J., 2, 4, 5, 9-15, 16, 24, 27, 28, 29, 31, 34, 38, 39, 52, 56,
    7∅, 73

Sartre, J-P., 3, 7, 8, 12, 15, 27, 35, 39, 42, 48, 52-56, 71, 72, 74, 75
Scheler, M., 18, 21, 74
Schelling, F.W.J., 23
Simon, B., 39
Simon, S., 58
Skinner, B.F., 3, 37, 46, 63, 64, 66-9, 71, 72, 73
Solomon, R., 46
Spinoza, B., 36, 62
Stevenson, C.L., 51
Strauss, L., 8

Talmon, J.L., 8, 15
Taylor, C., 3, 4, 8, 22
Telfer, E., 32, 58

Voegelin, E., 8, 63, 64, 66
Voltaire, 9, 1∅

White, J., 1, 49, 5∅, 51, 58
Wilson, E.O., 61
Wilson, J., 49, 5∅, 58, 59
Wolff, C., 16
Woods, R., 58, 59
Wordsworth, W., 2∅

Young, R., 17, 47, 49

82